*A
harvest
of ideas
for shooting
wonderful
color films
with any kind of
home movie
camera*

How to make GOOD

HOME

MOVIES

*by the
editors of
Eastman Kodak
Company*

Some of the products and services
mentioned in this book may not be
available outside the United States.

1966 Printing

Contents

Introduction

PART TWO *the why's and wherefore's*

Anything
is more fun
if you
start out with a bang!

• And if you have a choice, why not do it that way? After all, is there anyone who hates success? As Sophie Tucker once remarked, "I've been rich and I've been poor, but believe me, rich is better."

So, *How To Make Good Home Movies* is organized as two separate books in one. The first offers the quick and easy way. It encompasses the very least amount of information anyone would need to compile a good movie, not every possible kind of movie but the kind that beginners almost always start with and that most people shoot most of the time.

Part One isn't cluttered with unnecessary technicalities or with data that relates only to specialized types of moviemaking. After all, if you want to film some kids playing touch football on a bright sunny day, who cares *why* the correct lens setting is between 11 and 16, just as long as you know that it is the correct setting. In Part One the list of basic "things to remember" is trimmed to a manageable minimum. Once you've read it and go out to shoot a movie, you won't find yourself feeling like an apprentice juggler who has too many balls in the air.

Part Two covers the why's and wherefore's. It explains the reasoning behind most of the ideas you're asked to accept outright in Part One. But it includes much more. In it are relatively advanced moviemaking techniques, such as editing; it describes how to shoot movies in a wide range of unusual conditions and situations; it contains a collection of ideas you may wish to try as you become more experienced and confident.

The intent of this book, then, is to help you start at the top and then keep going up.

Chances are that you'll find one word used repeatedly on these pages in a way that doesn't jibe with your usual concept of it. This word is "scene." In a play or a commercial movie, a scene is a chain of action that occurs continuously in the same place at the same time. In talking about home movies though, it's more convenient to apply the term "scene" to the individual slice of action pictured each time you press and release the camera button. On a 50-foot roll of 8mm film, most people average about 24 home movie scenes (as the word is used in this book), but, if all of them show a baby being fed a single meal, the sum total might be only one scene of the other kind.

Chapter 1

Movies
*are different
from
still pictures*

Part I

Movies Show Actual Motion

The mantle of "World's Fastest Human" usually falls on an athlete who runs the 100-yard dash in a shade more than nine seconds. But if a normal boy or girl hangs his dungarees at your house, you may have a different candidate for the title. Most kids seem capable of turning in three laps around the living room in 0.0 seconds flat, with time included to upset a table lamp or a crystal vase.

Children move. Adults move, too, although generally at a less headlong pace. In this highly kinetic world of ours, nearly everything moves, and the recording of movement is a movie camera's chief *raison d'etre*.

Give a child a pogo stick, a snow shovel, a bicycle, or a cocker spaniel, and your snapshot camera will be able to freeze engaging and appealing slices of the reaction that occurs. With a movie camera, though, you can preserve the entire event, unfrozen and continuous, exactly as it happens.

Stiffly posing subjects, with or without feathered headress, belong in front of cigar stores, not movie cameras.

Stressing the fact that movies move may seem rather like pointing out that London is full of Englishmen; yet, owners of home movie equipment often transfer into their moviemaking unnecessary habits acquired in regular snapshooting. The most unnecessary is the concept of "hold it." To your movie camera, it doesn't make the slightest difference whether the small boy in front of its lens is stiffened into the pose of a Grenadier Guardsman or whether he's hopping around like a kangaroo. It *should* make a difference to you, though. Almost any still camera, even the least costly, can produce a bigger and often a better picture of something that will stay put than a movie camera. When you bought your movie camera, you were mostly purchasing its ability to record continuous action in full color, and if you use it consistently for less than this, you simply are not getting 100 percent value from your investment.

Movies are best and most interesting when they show people actually doing things rather than merely smiling or waving tamely at the camera. A baby's first awkward steps, your family's vacation activities, a friend on water skis — these are the kinds of subjects that make memorable movies.

Of course, not every scene you shoot can be brimming with motion. Some of the larger works of man and nature simply won't cooperate. But, whenever you place eye to viewfinder, if you think primarily in terms of recording natural, interesting activity, your films will become a marvelously rewarding, continuing source of deep pleasure.

Movies Can Provide a Connected Story

The individual movie scenes you shoot are as intimately connected as Siamese twins simply because they are attached and follow one another along to the end of the reel. This provides them with a marvelous talent for telling a story.

"Story," at least as we use the term here, doesn't imply the scenario-plus-direction kind of production on display at your local theater or more local TV set. What it does imply is that normal activity, the kind most people like to see in their home movies, proceeds in a natural, logical sequence which usually explains itself, and that a movie containing scenes taken during such activity just naturally tells a story.

For example, when a very small boy receives his first snow shovel, he's more than likely to go through a number of separate actions. To start, of course, he'll take it from the person who's bought it for him, probably with a good deal of delight. Then, carrying it over his shoulder, he'll tramp out into the snow looking for a good place to start shoveling. He'll experiment with it, probably discover that certain loads are beyond his capacity, and finally become a pretty proficient snow shoveler. In the course of all this, he's played out a natural, everyday, typical small boy story, admittedly a simple one, but a story nevertheless. If you've merely followed along with your movie camera, shooting a little of each chapter, varying the length of your scenes and your shooting distance, you'll find, much to your pleasure, that you've captured a wonderful slice of childhood, complete and continuous, in a way that will make it repeatedly enjoyable not only to you, yourself, but to the audiences of friends and relatives who'll also see it.

When you bathe a small boy, there's sure to be a natural story . . .

9

. . . and your movie camera will find one in almost any normal activity.

This story-telling talent of home movies isn't, by any means, an automatic feature. Unless you make some effort to take advantage of it, your reels can be little more than a string of moving snapshots, with nothing tying them together but their physical connection. If you produce the kind of films that switch abruptly from a shot of the baby crawling, to one of Dad washing his new car, to one of Mom pruning a shrub, back to the baby eating a handful of dirt, you're missing one of the nicest, most unique advantages of home movies.

Movies Are Inexpensive

In terms of what you get for what you pay, a color movie on KODACHROME Film turns out to be a remarkably economical form of picturetaking. The 50-foot reel of 8mm film that comes back to you from the processing laboratory will provide your screen with about four minutes of wonderfully lively action. Most moviemakers will break that four minutes up into approximately 24 separate scenes, each averaging 10 seconds in duration. If your camera is the type that takes its 8mm film in roll form, each of those 24 scenes will cost you about as much as one-and-a-half ordinary black-and-white snapshot prints; if you buy your film in the slightly more expensive KODAPAK Cartridge loads, the cost per scene will about equal that of two black-and-white prints.

A 50-foot roll or magazine of 16mm KODACHROME Film will project for about two minutes and contain, on the average, about a dozen scenes. The cost per 16mm scene is just about the same as that of shooting two color slides.

10

Chapter II

Tips
for
getting started
quickly

Before an airline pilot takes off, he goes over a checklist to make sure everything is in order. Before you make movies, you should do the same thing. This chapter is your "preshooting" checklist. After you've shot a roll or two, you'll do these things as automatically as you put on your shoes.

Load Your Camera Properly

This is especially important if it's of the roll-film type. Light leaking into the edges of a roll of film when you load it causes orange streaks along the edges of the film. Cameras using super 8 film, such as KODAK INSTAMATIC Cameras, use factory-loaded cartridges of film that simply drop into place without any threading or film handling. No matter what kind of camera you have, follow the directions in your camera's instruction manual. If you've misplaced the manual, request another one from the camera's manufacturer. Be sure to specify exactly what type and model of camera you have.

You never touch the film when loading a KODAK INSTAMATIC *Movie Camera. Just drop in or push in the* KODAPAK *Movie Cartridge (front side first), depending on which camera model you have. Loading the camera automatically sets the film-footage indicator.*

Use the Right Kind of Film

Daylight and the light from movie lights used indoors aren't the same color. Daylight is bluish and artificial light is yellowish. A separate film is made for each type of light. Daylight Type film is, not surprisingly, for use in daylight. Type A film is for use with photoflood or "sun gun" lights. (The "A" stands for artificial light.) You can also use Type A film outdoors *if* you use a KODAK No. 85 Filter over the lens. In fact, *all* KODAK film currently made for KODAK INSTAMATIC Movie Cameras is Type A — and putting the KODAPAK Film Cartridge into the camera automatically positions such a filter in front of the lens for outdoor shooting. *(There's more film information on page 83.)*

Use the Right Lens Openings

Most modern movie cameras have automatic exposure-control mechanisms that set the proper lens opening for you. If your camera is of the manual, set-it-yourself kind, make your first couple of movies in bright sunlight. It's easy to recognize and produces brilliant colors. With KODACHROME II Movie Film for Daylight, set your lens between 11 and 16.

Bright or hazy sunlight can be recognized from the shadows it makes.

Hold Your Camera Correctly

Different movie cameras, like different fraternities, require different grips. See your instruction booklet for the correct way to hold your camera. Unless the camera is firmly and comfortably nestled in your hands, your movies may look as if they've been shot from a storm-tossed rowboat. Hold the camera tightly against your cheek, with your arms close to your

12

What looks like this . . .

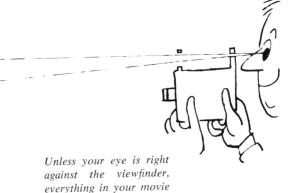

. . . turns out like this.

Unless your eye is right against the viewfinder, everything in your movie will be smaller and farther away than you intended.

body and your elbows pointed down. As a general rule, the *subjects* should move, not the camera. When you follow skiing, running, boating, or similar action, keep the moving subject centered in the viewfinder as you pivot smoothly from the waist. Otherwise, hold the camera still. *Waving your camera around as though it were the nozzle of a garden hose is the biggest single mistake in home movies.* The steadier, the better. The best movies are shot from a tripod. If you don't have one or won't use one, hold the camera s-t-e-a-d-y.

Keep the Camera Close to Your Eye

You should be able to see the entire area of the viewfinder frame. If your eye is too far away, everything in your movie will appear smaller and farther away than it looked through the viewfinder. Center your eye so that you're looking right through the center of the viewfinder, not from one side or the other. A movie camera is like a gun—you have to aim properly to get what you shoot.

Panning with a moving subject makes the background blurry, but keeps the moving subject fairly sharp. If you must pan with scenic subjects, move the camera very slowly.

Camera Focusing

Most 8mm movie cameras have fixed-focus lenses, set at the factory to make acceptably sharp pictures from a few feet away to as far as you can see. Don't get closer to the subject than your instruction manual says you can. If your camera *does* have a focusing scale, be sure to set it for the distance between the camera and the subject before every shot. Be especially careful to focus correctly when you're using a zoom lens at its telephoto position. *(There's more on focusing on page 94.)*

Your Camera's Motor

Every movie camera has either a wind-up spring motor or an electric motor to drive the film. If you have a spring-driven motor, wind it before you start shooting and after each scene. Then you won't find yourself in the middle of an important scene with a run-down motor. Cameras with electric motors never need winding, but they do need batteries. Use alkaline batteries and replace them once each year. Take the batteries out of your camera if you don't plan to use it for several months. *(See page 162 for more on camera care.)*

Camera Speeds

Film travels through most movie cameras at a rate of about 18 frames per second. When you project your film at the same speed, action appears normal on the screen. Movies taken at slower-than-usual speeds give speeded-up, choppy movement on the screen for comedy effects. Movies taken at faster than the normal rate produce slow-motion effects on the screen. Cameras with adjustable speeds are usually marked with two or more of these numbers: 8, 16, 24, 32, and 64. These refer to frames per second. Camera speeds other than the normal 16 or 18 frames per second require different lens openings than normal. *(Camera speeds are discussed in more detail on page 96.)*

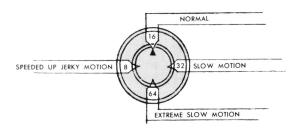

15

Chapter **III**

*Making
an
outdoor movie*

Start with color, add plenty of action, and, chances are, you'll have a good movie.

Getting Started the Easy Way

You've probably already equipped yourself, courtesy of the previous chapter, with a brief mental checklist for simplified outdoor moviemaking.

- bright sunlight
- camera loaded with appropriate film
- lens set at right opening
- focus at proper distance
- camera speed at 16 frames per second

All to the good. But items like correct exposure and sharp focus are only mechanical factors, certainly important, but still purely mechanical. The most accurately exposed home movie ever made might also be the dullest. The vital ingredients for a good film are the action occurring in front of the camera and the thought processes occurring behind it.

17

Few people enter upon home movie shooting out of any fatal fascination with the photographic details of it. Usually the impetus is the simple desire to preserve things — perhaps the pageant of a vacation trip or the doings of a growing family. Most of us want good movies, but we want to achieve them without the fuss that would make our camera a constant and annoying preoccupation. The question, though, is "How?"

Knowing a little about shooting good movies really starts with knowing a little about people and the way they react to the presence of any device photographic. To only the most youthful or the most misanthropic, is a camera inconsequential. When most others become aware that a camera's unblinking stare is aimed in their direction, they react stiffly, self-consciously, and inhibitedly. To capture them unself-conscious and relatively uninhibited, your best bet is to plan your shooting for occasions when your intended subjects are engrossed in some sort of activity.

This offers two advantages of no mean proportion. First, a person who's interested in whatever he's doing isn't likely to be bothered much by a camera. In addition, natural activities imply some sort of natural story pattern, and a story, no matter how rudimentary, is a tremendous asset to any movie.

So, before you start to shoot, think. Instead of simply deciding point blank to make a movie of your family, for example, hold your fire until they are engaged in some movie-worthy activity. If one doesn't begin spontaneously, launch it yourself.

Putting a Movie Together

Let's say you've picked up a roll of film that you'd like to use during the weekend. You know some friends are due over for an afternoon cookout. Save your film for this. Here's how you might make such a movie without your becoming a nuisance to the rest of the group and without the camera's becoming a nuisance to you.

A good story starts by setting the scene, so you could first shoot an overall view of your back yard and house, preferably with some member of your family working around it, as someone undoubtedly would be, getting ready for the cookout. This immediately establishes where the action is going to take place and need consume only about 6 to 10 seconds. You might then move in for a closer shot to show exactly what kind of work the person is doing, whether it be setting up the table or dumping charcoal into the grill.

When your guests arrive, perhaps toting the dessert or some other contribution, you might try shooting some footage of

A country fair? Take your camera. And for a colorful finale, the hustling trotters and silks of their drivers.

Whenever your movie camera accompanies you to any sort of special event, even one that generates as much tension as a sports car race, be sure to aim it occasionally at some of the sidelights. Scenes of the careening cars will seem even more exciting when interspersed with brief views of the anxious pit crews and the spectators.

them without tipping them off, but there's always a chance that the first awareness of the camera might cause them to freeze in their tracks and merely gape at it. This is one type of shot that is often better if "semiacted" rather than photographed impromptu.

Eventually, someone will light the fire (a good spot for a brief, very close close-up showing just hands, match, and charcoal) and then, more than likely, the chef will make his entrance, perhaps in the uniform of his calling and carrying a platter of succulent steaks — or are they hamburgers? Whatever the fare may be, when he places the meat on the grill, bring the camera close enough so it can really see what he's about and then move it much, much closer for a view of the red, marbled steaks (or hamburgers) sizzling over the fire or being turned.

At a range of 3½ feet, your movie camera covers an area of about this size. You can exploit its close-up shooting ability by closing in on faces or filling the screen with important details.

This, again, might be only a brief scene but will add variety and help tie the story together. Close-ups of this sort and of people are the true spice of home moviemaking, the element that gives it a unique visual impact. Perhaps the greatest fault in most home movies is that they lack sufficient close-ups. Even with inexpensive, nonfocusing equipment, you can get sharp movies from as near as 3½ feet on a bright sunny day. At this range the camera eye takes in an area only about 10 by 15 inches.

Once the food is served, detach yourself momentarily from your own plate for a scene or two of the entire group at the table. If you'd like, you can even get into the picture yourself. Most cameras have a lock adjustment on the camera button which will keep the camera running without a finger actually pressed over the button. Just set the camera on some firm support—a table or chair will do if you don't have a tripod—aim it, lock the button, and join the rest of the party. After a few seconds, get up, walk outside the area covered by the camera lens, approach the camera, and release the button.

Eating time is also a good time for close-ups of each person at the table, especially the kids if there are any. It's always fun to see a small girl tackling a large hot dog or an eager boy burrowing into an oversized slice of watermelon.

On most cameras the button can be locked in the "on" position, enabling you to get in the picture, by pressing it a notch farther than normal.

Whatever the program after dinner, whether it's merely sitting around companionably over a tall drink or working off the effects of overeating with a bit of croquet, badminton, or softball, it, too, belongs in your movie.

By the time your guests leave or it simply has become too late in the day for good color shots of people (usually a couple of hours before sunset), you'll have collected much more than a mere hodgepodge of isolated moving snapshots. Inside your camera, imprisoned on the film and ready for processing, is a truly documentary film story of the cookout, just as it happened. If you've remembered to vary camera-to-subject distances and scene lengths, and to include an ample sampling of close-ups, it's certain to be a continuing source of pleasure for many years to come.

Variety and Accurate Exposure

Of course, this isn't a formula for making a movie of a picnic or cookout. It's simply an example of the kind of scenes that will add up to a good film and how they can be put together so as to have an interesting continuity.

Both scene length and subject distance are topics that come in for a more exhaustive treatment in Chapter IX (page 100), but the central point about both is that they should be varied from one scene to another whenever possible. Some activities deserve 15 seconds of camera time, while others can be covered neatly in 5. It's hardly ever necessary to shoot a single burst much longer than 15 seconds in duration. Instead, cover a continuous activity in brief scenes made from several different distances and angles. This not only economizes on film but produces a livelier, less static movie.

Automatic Cameras

With an automatic camera, just aim and shoot. Try to have the sun shining directly on the subject. You can also make pleasing movies with the sun to one side or ahead of you, as long as sunlight isn't falling directly on the lens or meter. Don't shoot subjects that are partly in sunlight and partly in shade. They should be completely in sunlight or completely in shade. A warning signal appears in the viewfinder when there's not enough light to make good movies.

Manually Set Cameras

It's quite desirable to make your first few outdoor movies in bright sunshine, not only because it produces bright colors but because it is a lighting condition extremely easy to identify.

The only important adjustment you need make for bright sunshine shooting occurs when you are photographing scenery that doesn't include nearby people but does contain large areas of light sand or snow. The setting for this kind of subject should be one stop smaller than normal. Often, though, an event or a

An overcast day — but an only chance. Just open the lens three full openings more than for a sunlit subject.

In bright sun, subjects containing large areas of light sand, snow, or glaring water and without people in the close foreground should be photographed at a lens opening one stop smaller than normal. Automatic cameras will automatically make this adjustment.

good movie opportunity will occur in other than bright sun and can't be postponed. To shoot movies under other classifications of daylight, it's only necessary to use the right lens setting. These classifications are defined on page 86. The settings recommended for them with KODACHROME II Film are also shown on the same page.

The big difference between movies and still pictures is that movies move. Include plenty of action in your films, not people staring self-consciously into the camera.

WAR IN THE SNOW

Anyone can make a movie of a gang of boys standing around and looking uncomfortable. Chances are that confronted by a movie camera this is just about what most boys would normally do. But if in the midst of some activity of their own choosing or one you've prodded them into for your own devious purposes—a snowball fight, for instance—they probably won't be inhibited by the camera and may add a little extra enthusiasm to their efforts, hams that they are. It's important, though, to keep the camera on the sidelines. In a snowball fight, of course, you may be klonked on the back of the head if you don't. But in anything going along under its own steam, if you intrude too much or try to direct too much, it's likely to lose all of its genuine flavor and the result won't have the really memorable quality that spells out "B-O-Y."

When our boys pack up for a war in the snow, they equip for a major engineering project.

Of course, Steve and John are willing to let Gerry do the heavy labor, as long as he insists.

Since Tom is the architect of the defensive works, he gets to lay the cornerstone.

That's Gerry smoothing down the frontal armor plate, with his brother Hank in the background.

By now the fort is beginning to take on a fairly formidable appearance . . .

. . . although it's not nearly as high as desired, . . .

. . . especially by Tom, who'll settle for nothing less than complete protection.

Finally it's time to stock up the defender's armory . . .

. . . and Tom figures on prolonged hostilities.

Charge!

Hank and Steve get ready . . .

. . . and let go with a barrage.

But Tom has a small barrage of his own ready to launch . . .

. . . and Steve receives a direct hit.

As with most fortifications, one dent generally . . .

. . . leads to others . . .

. . . and although the defensive troops still have plenty of fight left in them, . . .

. . . as Steve can testify (that Steve, he always gets it). . . .

. . . the victors really rub it in with a vengeance.

And that, as Tom and Gerry are willing to admit, is that.

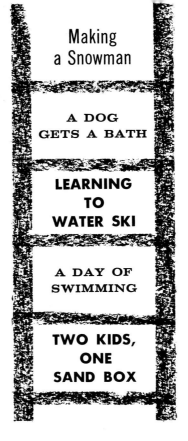

Making
a Snowman

A DOG
GETS A BATH

LEARNING
TO
WATER SKI

A DAY OF
SWIMMING

TWO KIDS,
ONE
SAND BOX

A Few Examples

The ideas you'll find here aren't meant as scripts. Most really good home movies aren't the fruit of scripts anyway, but rather of things photographed as they happened and logically linked together. These ideas are simply examples of the kinds of scenes which would contribute to a pleasant movie record of the overall activity during which they'd occurred. They certainly won't fit everyone or, perhaps, anyone. When your family goes to the beach, it's possible that the youngest offspring, rather than needing any swimming instruction from you, may know and use more strokes than a duffer in a sand trap. But if none of these collections applies strictly to your own shooting, they may offer some ideas you'll find highly useful. For vacation films, you'll also find many helpful hints in Chapter XII, beginning on page 140.

Making a Snowman

- *The kids and one parent come trooping out into the park or onto the lawn*
- *The parent shows them how to roll the big snowballs needed for a snowman*
- *Close-up of a child's hands starting to roll a snowball*
- *The parent, with help from the kids, stacks the large snowballs to form the body and head*
- *Close-up of one of the kids making the face*
- *The arms are stuck into the body and someone adds a hat for a debonair touch*
- *The sculptors pose, probably mugging, with their work of art*

The Dog Gets a Bath

- *Close-up shows water from a garden hose being run into a large tub or child's wading pool*
- *Someone pours bubble bath into the water and stirs it up*
- *One of the family calls the dog and he comes bounding into view.*
- *Attempts are made to lure the dog into the bath*
- *He is finally dragged in bodily*
- *Medium-length and close-up shots of the dog undergoing his trial by soap and water*
- *Finally released from the bath, the dog is swabbed with towels*
- *He ends matters by shaking water all over his bathers*

You can get good color movies even if your subject isn't in the sun. For data on open shade shooting, see page 86.

A movie needn't show every bit of an activity. Scenes of the high spots tell the story.

A bucking horse spells "rodeo" better than any view of a grandstand. A football scrimmage or "tractor driver" spells "boy" as no tame version can. Your movie camera delivers the greatest dividends when trained on action.

Learning to Water Ski

- *Someone far out on the lake comes skiing toward the camera*
- *He comes in to shore, kicks off his skis, and talks some member of the family into trying it*
- *Medium-length and close-up shots show the neophyte receiving preliminary instructions*
- *The pupil puts on his skis, the boat pulls away, and, more than likely, he falls down*
- *After several other unsuccessful tries, he finally manages to stay on his feet*
- *The photographer gets into the boat and shoots some footage of the new water skier in action*
- *The boat pulls back into shore*
- *Close-up shows the new skier happily mopping himself off with a towel*

A Day of Swimming

- *The family loading the car with food, beach equipment, blankets*
- *Scenery along the way and the approaches to the lake or ocean can be shot directly through the front windshield while the car is moving*

- *The children running down the shore and splashing into the water*
- *Swimming instruction for the smallest child, with close-ups of the neophyte merman or mermaid*
- *Lunchtime*
- *Shots of the members of the family using floats or inflatable animals or engaged in water fights*
- *Special stunts, such as one of the kids diving off dad's shoulders*
- *Wet swimmers flinging themselves onto the blanket for a session of sun worship*
- *Packing up the equipment and reloading it into the car for the trip home*

Two Kids, One Sandbox

- *The children carrying pails, shovels, and other toys, coming out of the house or garage*
- *Making cakes, undertaking construction projects, and producing other creative achievements with close-ups of the handiwork*
- *Not-so-creative achievements, like shampooing each other's hair with sand*
- *Mother drags the kids out of the sandbox and performs on-the-spot cleanup*

Every trip to a photo-scenic locale isn't a honeymoon, but every sightseeing film you shoot can take advantage of the ideas in this movie story (it has about as many scenes as you can get comfortably into a roll of 8mm film) for showing place, people at place, and ending up with a pleasant, natural narrative. The initial scene is an overall view of the American Falls. The next two show the bride getting a more intimate look. Then the camera peers down at the wooden catwalk of the Cave of the Winds and, immediately after, you have the slightly damp couple trudging along that catwalk. Each time, the film displays the locale first, then the people in it. By the way, if you should want your entire party in some scenes as the couple is here, just set the camera and ask a friendly-looking bystander if he'll do the shooting. You'll hardly ever get a turndown.

You just hear it first, but suddenly there it is, looking like every post-card of it you've ever seen.

Anne wanted the bird's-eye view, but you'll notice that she didn't let go of that railing.

She decided that the telescope was a safer way of getting a close look than going over in a barrel.

That spindly-looking structure down below is the catwalk at the Cave of the Winds.

It was with no few trepidations that we decided to try it out.

Actually it isn't as rickety as it looks—nothing could be.

When you see all that water, you feel a strong impulse to get back to solid ground.

Needless to say, despite the slickers, it gets dampish down there under the Falls.

The border runs along the middle of the river and across the middle of the bridge . . .

. . . and so before you leave the span, you encounter Canadian Customs.

The Customs Officer sees so many honeymooners that he doesn't even crack jokes.

He cleared us politely and rapidly and sent us on our way.

After checking in at the hotel, we felt like taking a quick tour around the Canadian side.

We ran into a policeman . . .

. . . who suggested that we might
be likely to enjoy . . .

. . . a ride in a surrey, complete
with fringe and friendly driver.

Anne discussed routing with him
and told him that all we wanted
to see was everything.

He helped her in and away we
clip-clopped.

A horsedrawn pace is ideal for
viewing the Falls. It gives you
time to gauge their size.

And anyway, someone's got to
support the horse.

A Parade

- *Shots of the crowd waiting along both sides of the street*
- *The vanguard of the parade moving toward your stationary camera*
- *Different elements of the parade, bands, floats, drill teams, as they go by — you can follow them by swinging around slowly with your camera, making the swivel from your waist*
- *Side action such as the expressions on children's faces, vendors selling balloons, food, and souvenirs — these scenes can be interspersed with scenes of the actual parade*
- *The last marching unit going by and the crowd streaming out into the street*

A Scenic Trip

- *Shoot through the window of your train, plane, or bus as it pulls away from your home departure point as long as it isn't shaded or indoors*
- *Get scenes of any interesting scenery you pass, shooting through the window or windshield of your plane, train, bus, or car*

- *Close-ups of signs describing any scenic attractions followed up by views of the attractions themselves*
- *Shoot extremely tall objects, such as skyscrapers, waterfalls, or sequoia trees by starting either at the top or bottom and then moving the camera very, very slowly toward the opposite extremity*
- *Get close-ups and medium-distance shots of members of your party engaged in characteristic activities; for example, riding burros down into Grand Canyon, feeding the pelicans at St. Petersburg, or buying souvenirs anywhere*
- *Include informal activities, such as picnics, swimming, feeding birds, and animals*

Review of Camera Settings

Lens opening: determines whether movies and their colors will be dark, natural-looking, or light; the numbers may have an f in front of them; they will usually be in a series like 1.9, 2.8, 4, 5.6, 8, 11, 16, although the first number might be 2.3 or 2.7; the smallest numbers are the largest openings.

Focus: determines whether the subject will appear sharp and distinct or fuzzy and indistinct; on many cameras it is preset for maximum range of sharpness; the settings will almost always be in terms of feet.

Camera speed: determines whether motion will be shown normally, more slowly than normally, or faster than normal; many cameras are preset at 16 or 18 frames per second, normal speed for silent movies; some cameras offer a choice of speeds, usually from among 8, 16, 24, 48, and 64 frames per second.

Chapter IV

Making an indoor movie

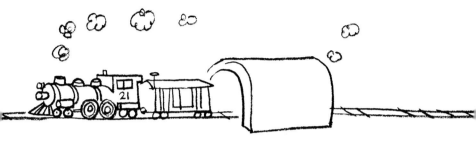

Indoor Movie Opportunities

Once there were a brother and sister, both of tender years, who, after a simply exhausting day of snacking on homemade mud pies, rolling in piles of grass clippings, and engaging in other delightful but equally grimy pastimes, were marched energetically into the bathroom for their communal scrubdown. Here they competed in brisk undressing contests, hurled themselves into the tub with great enthusiasm, shampooed each other with extremely soapy water, conducted boat races in which both cheated shamefully, and left their bespattered parents amused, exhausted, and totally unconscious that such carryings-on make wonderful home movies.

Unfortunately, many movie cameras lead a neglected indoor life because their owners aren't conscious of the opportunities for good movies that constantly surround them. Parents who faithfully chronicle the outdoor activities of their families often forget that much of a child's life occurs indoors, that birthdays are movie-worthy occasions, and that Christmas and other holidays inevitably sneak around every 365 days or so. Many people who wouldn't be parted from their movie cameras on a vacation trip somehow ignore them for weddings and parties. If it were more difficult or considerably more costly to shoot indoor movies, this might be understandable, but actually it's neither.

A movie camera outdoors is a relatively inconspicuous item. Indoors, though, its attendant photoflood lamps are a constant source of distraction to the people you photograph. For best results, they should be shown in some sort of interesting activities and encouraged to perform those activities as if the camera wasn't looking in.

There's at least one instance in which home movies have a certain advantage over the original event — aspiring young trumpet players are seen, but not heard.

Electrical Sunlight

There's one big difference between outdoor and indoor moviemaking. Outdoors, nature supplies the light. Indoors, you provide it by means of movie lights. The ordinary lights in your home produce plenty of light for life's normal activities, but they're too dim for making color movies. This shortcoming is remedied by a device that holds a high-intensity light right on your camera. You simply plug the cord into a convenient outlet, click the switch, and you're directing a strong beam of light wherever you aim your camera.

There are various kinds of movie lights—lamps with built-in reflectors that screw into a light bar, sealed-beam units, and "sun gun" units. All of them seem extremely bright when you switch them on in a normally-lit room. They're not as bright as they seem. Two photofloods held at arm's length, for example, deliver no more light to your face than sunlight does on a bright day. One good technique is to aim the lights toward the ceiling when you turn them on. Then, after a few seconds, point them at your subject and they won't seem so brilliant.

Use Type A Film

To get the right color balance in your movies, use Type A film with movie lights. If you use Daylight Type film with movie lights, your pictures will be too yellowish. *All* KODAK film sold for use in KODAK INSTAMATIC Movie Cameras (and other cameras using super 8 film) is Type A. To make indoor movies with an INSTAMATIC Movie Camera, you must first remove the daylight conversion filter that's normally over the lens. There are two ways to remove the filter: When you attach a KODAK INSTAMATIC Movie Light to the camera, it automatically removes the filter; or, if you're using some other kind of movie light, insert the filter key supplied with the camera and push it down to remove the filter.

Exposure and Shooting Distances

When you make indoor movies with a light on the camera, *the lens setting depends on the distance from the light to the subject.* If your camera has lens openings you set yourself, this bit of information is all-important. It means that *every time you change your shooting distance, you must also change your lens opening.* The exact lens opening to use for various distances is found in film instruction sheets, on most movie lights, and in the table on page 49 of this book.

The more accurate your estimates of distance, the better your exposures will be. You don't have to be "on the nose." If your subject is 10 feet away and you guess wrong by a foot or two in either direction, it won't make too much difference. One good way of guessing distances is to imagine your own height laid out on the ground, and to measure mentally in terms of one, one-and-a-half, or two body lengths.

Automatic Cameras

To use an automatic camera indoors with a movie light, just set the film-speed dial to 40 for KODACHROME II Movie Film, Type A. (Even this is unnecessary with KODAK INSTAMATIC Movie Cameras.) You don't have to judge the shooting distance, because your camera's meter will automatically select the right lens opening for the brightness of the scene. Try to keep your subjects within a few feet of the background. Otherwise, the meter will "see" a dark area behind the subject, open the lens too wide, and cause overexposure of the subject itself.

Attaching a KODAK INSTAMATIC *Movie Light to your* KODAK INSTAMATIC *Movie Camera automatically removes a filter from in front of the lens so that you can make movies indoors.*

Some Details about Movie Lights

There are several kinds of lights designed for indoor movie-making. All of them have built-in reflectors to concentrate the light on your subject. With movie light bars, you'll need reflector-type photoflood lamps marked BEP, EBR, or BFA. These lamps produce about the same amount of light, but differ in size and the amount of current they consume. As this type of lamp burns, it gets progressively weaker. After one hour of lamp life, for example, you must use a lens opening one-half bigger than you'd need for new lamps. After two hours, you need a whole lens opening bigger. If you have an automatic camera, you don't have to worry about this, because your camera will compensate for such lamp changes automatically.

47

If you use a conventional movie light, use the special filter key supplied with your KODAK INSTAMATIC *Movie Camera to move the filter aside before making indoor movies.*

The light from photoflood lamps won't harm normal eyesight. But splashing cold liquids on hot lamps may cause them to explode, so be careful.

Another type of light source is used in the KODAK INSTAMATIC Movie Light. Instead of several reflector-type photoflood lamps, it uses a single, high-intensity lamp in a compact reflector unit. It has several advantages over conventional photoflood lamps. It's smaller, burns many times longer, doesn't change light output with use, and requires less current to operate. There's also a built-in "danger signal." When the gas in the lamp is pinkish, the lamp is too hot to touch. When the gas regains its original clarity, it's cool. This type of lamp produces so much light and heat that *you shouldn't use them closer than six feet to the subject.*

INDOOR EXPOSURE TABLE

KODACHROME II Movie Film, Type A		
Lens Opening	KODAK INSTAMATIC Movie Light	2-Lamp Bar Light with 300- or 375-watt (BEP or BFA) Reflector Photo Lamps*
f8		3½— 5 feet
f5.6	6 feet	5— 7 feet
f4	8 feet	7—10 feet
f2.8	10 feet	10—14 feet
f1.9	16 feet	15—21 feet

*For new lamps, beams superimposed. After they have burned for 1 hour, use lens opening ½ stop wider; after 2 hours, use next-wider opening.

Bounce Lighting

Lights attached to your camera and aimed directly at the subject produce flat, even illumination. The illumination is strong, but not always pleasing for all subjects. One way to produce more natural lighting effects is to aim your movie light at the ceiling so that illumination is reflected back down onto the scene. This technique, called "bounce" lighting, lights up the whole room instead of just one spot, and produces softer, more diffuse lighting.

Some movie lights are purposely made to swivel upward just for this purpose. But you can have someone point any movie light toward the ceiling, or even prop it on books atop a TV set or piano so that its beam is aimed upward. In small rooms with deep colors, you may get a color cast on the film with bounce lighting.

Automatic cameras set themselves for any type of lighting. It's slightly trickier when you have to set the lens yourself. As a rule of thumb, you should get acceptable results in most rooms with white ceilings by using an exposure of f1.9 with KODACHROME II Movie Film, Type A, and a KODAK INSTAMATIC Movie Light. One big exposure bonus of bounce lighting is that you don't have to change the lens setting every time you move.

49

CLOSING IN ON A BABY FACE

The expressions that wrinkle across a baby's face, from the stormiest to the sublimest, are all quite wonderful. Be sure to do much of your baby filming close up (but not closer than 6 feet with a "sun-gun" type of movie light). If you give the baby time to become accustomed to the lights, chances are that they won't bother him.

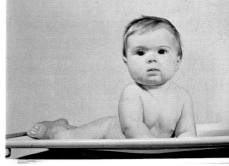

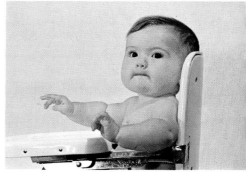

Indoor Movies with Off-Camera Lights

Sun guns and bar lights attached to the camera provide the easiest way of making indoor movies. But to show off your subject to the best advantage or to obtain special lighting effects, you may want to use your lights off the camera. You can put your photoflood lamps into inexpensive clip-on units that clamp to a chair, table, or banister, or have someone hold your sun gun wherever you want it.

The advantage of this type of lighting is that the lights and shadows look more natural. The disadvantages are that it's more cumbersome to set up and that the exposures are harder to figure (unless you have an automatic camera).

Here's a good arrangement for getting started. Set up one light near the camera and slightly above it. Put the second lamp out at an angle of 45° to the camera-subject axis, as shown in the illustration. It should be about two feet higher than your subject's head and a little closer than the other light. Superimpose the beams of both lamps on the subject. For even better results, shine a third light on the wall behind the subject. With this kind of setup, you can move around with your camera without having to change the lens opening. (The distance from the

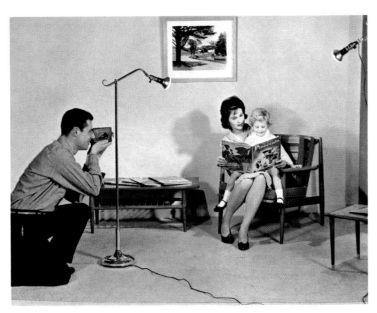

lights to the subject is fixed in this case, so you always use the same exposure.) You can study the effects and move the lights around until you find the result you like best. Make sure there are no unshaded lamps glaring into your camera lens.

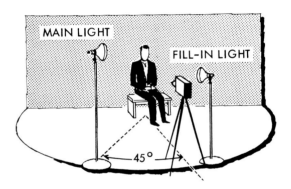

A Basic Two-Light Arrangement

A simple, but effective, fixed lighting arrangement can be set up by putting one light (the "fill-in" light) at the camera, and another (the "main" light) high and to one side. The main light should be placed at a 45-degree angle from the line between the subject and the camera. These lights should be at the right distance to illuminate the highlights in the face without "burning out" the modeling. The Flood Light Dial in the *Kodak Master Photoguide* gives exposure data for this type of simple lighting arrangement. With movie cameras, use the lens settings opposite 1/30 second. Photoflood lamps have guide numbers, just as flashbulbs do, and provide another way of determining exposure. Meters give the most accurate results.

There's no use ignoring the all-too-obvious fact that most adults feel somewhat ill at ease in the bright beam of a movie light bar. They're less uncomfortable, though, when doing something with a child and especially when in a completely relaxed situation, such as a party.

▶

When boy meets bologna sandwich, especially small boy and large sandwich, the movie potentialities are measureless. Children at mealtime are always first-rate movie subjects and easy ones, chiefly because they stay put. ▶

54

Getting Down to the Shooting

To see how all of this works in practice, let's say that some very young person in whom you have an interest is about to be fed his breakfast. Even before he's deposited in his high chair or at his feeder table, turn your photofloods on so that he'll become adjusted to their presence. Then, when his meal is ready, pick up your camera and step back far enough for an overall view of his mother bibbing him and presenting him with his cereal.

The distance might be about 12 or 13 feet. With a manual camera, check the table on your light bar to find the right lens opening. Focus, if your camera requires it, and shoot 8 to 10 seconds' worth to launch the story. Then, move in closer, perhaps to 9 feet, so that you can catch his efforts to maneuver spoon into mouth. After several bursts, during which your small subject probably coats his outside with as much cereal as he does his inside, you might move in for a close-up of his oatmeal-encrusted face.

Once you've become accustomed to changing openings every time you or your subject changes position, the rest of the routine for a good movie will be just as it was outdoors — shoot natural activity, vary distance and scene length frequently, include plenty of close-ups, and try to tell a story.

The only important booby-trap unique to indoor shooting is that extremely reflective, shiny surfaces can hurl big glare spots back into your lens. If a mirror or some other glossy surface is close behind your subject, always shoot from at least a 45-degree angle to this surface so that the reflection will be outside the picture area.

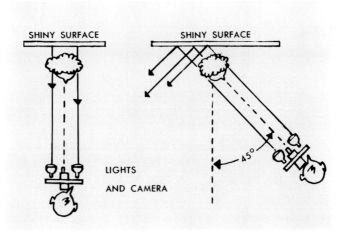

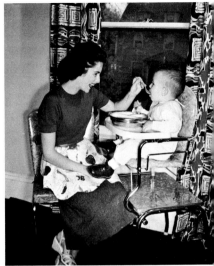

When the beams of your photoflood lamps are aimed directly into any highly reflective surface, the flaring reflection will spoil the entire movie scene. If there should be some glass or a similar material in the background of a scene, move your shooting position around to one side so that when you look through the camera finder, you don't see your own image or that of the lights.

A Few Examples

You may not have a batheable baby, an all-consuming passion for model trains, or the slightest desire to officiate at an adult party celebrating Halloween. Be that as it may, the ideas listed on pages 62 and 63 could help you acquire a better appreciation of how to assemble a good indoor movie reel about some subject in which you are interested. If you should be planning to capture on film your small one's next soap-and-water stint, your miniature "iron horse" in action, or a forthcoming Halloween divertissement, many of these suggested scenes may work out very nicely for you.

LAURA'S SEVENTH BIRTHDAY

Any movie of a birthday party could hardly avoid being a sheer delight, but if it starts with the party proper it may miss fully half of the fun. In the twenty scenes of this birthday story—a number of scenes, by the way, that you can easily make on a single roll of 8mm film—the first nine show the preparations for the party and only the last eleven the party itself. In shooting movies of other special events, you'll invariably find that the film will turn out to be more interesting if you do begin with the groundwork. At Thanksgiving, instead of making your first scenes at the dinner table, begin in the kitchen several hours earlier. At Christmas, rather than shooting the initial scenes on the morning of the twenty-fifth, devote a portion of your film to the trimming of the tree the night before.

58

Of course the invitations had gone out in the mail a week before, but Laura just had to double check.

Cake icing is always a source of great interest and, as usual, there was no dearth of help for Mother.

It was quite a race to see if Laura could ice the cake before sister Gail iced her stomach.

Laura counted twice, just to make sure there were seven.

Spectator response became a shade apathetic at times, but . . .

She also served as assistant interior decorator.

. . . there was plenty of activity when it came time to stick the candles in.

Heaven knows, a young lady has to look glamorous on her very own seventh birthday . . .

. . . but this hundred strokes business is simply ridiculous.

But it all turned out to be very much worthwhile, . . .

. . . although it was sometimes hard to tell whose gifts they were supposed to be.

After a brief time out for a bit of girlish chit-chat, . . .

. . . Pin-The-Tail-On-The-Donkey became the chief attraction . . .

. . . with the usual rather low level of marksmanship.

The only way to stop a sudden outbreak of balloon batting was to announce cake and ice cream.

First, of course, there had to be a chorus of "Happy Birthday" . . .

. . . and the other usual formalities, such as cake cutting . . .

. . . and favor opening.

A good time was had by all.

Well, nearly all.

Baby Takes a Bath

- *Close-up of water being poured into the tub, dishpan, or bathinette*
- *Baby being lifted by its mother out of the crib or playpen*
- *Scenes, from varying distances and angles, of the baby being undressed*
- *Medium-distance scene of the baby being lowered gently into the water*
- *Close-up of the baby's face to catch his reaction*
- *Medium-distance scenes of the baby being washed and of him splashing and playing*
- *Baby being taken out of the water and wrapped in a towel*
- *Close-up of the baby's face while he is being dried and his hair combed*
- *Baby being dressed and then given his bottle*

Model Trains in Action

- *Close-up of an engine as smoke starts to puff out of its smokestack and it slowly begins to move forward*
- *Medium-distance scenes of the train running through the layout*
- *Close-ups of such accessory items as a crossing gate closing and then the train racing past*
- *Brief scene showing boy or man in engineer's cap operating the transformer and remote-control equipment*

- *Close-up of a tunnel, with the train suddenly bursting out of it*
- *Scenes of the train pulling into the freight yard*
- *Close-ups of special gadgets at work, such as automatic freight car loaders, crane cars, and coal loaders*
- *The human engineer finally stops the train and turns off all of his battery of electrical equipment*

A Halloween Party for Adults

- *Brief scenes of costumed guests being greeted at the door by the hostess or host*
- *Close-up of hand ladling a cup of cider or punch from bowl*
- *Guests sitting around drinking cider or punch*
- *Scenes of different guests struggling through games, with many close-ups of faces as people bob for apples, squirm under the barrier in low-crawling contest, or exhibit confusion while trying to pin-the-tail-on-the-donkey*
- *Overall scene as some dancing commences*
- *Medium-distance scenes of people with incongruous or clumsy costumes trying to dance with each other*
- *Final scene of everyone in the kitchen for an impromptu snack*

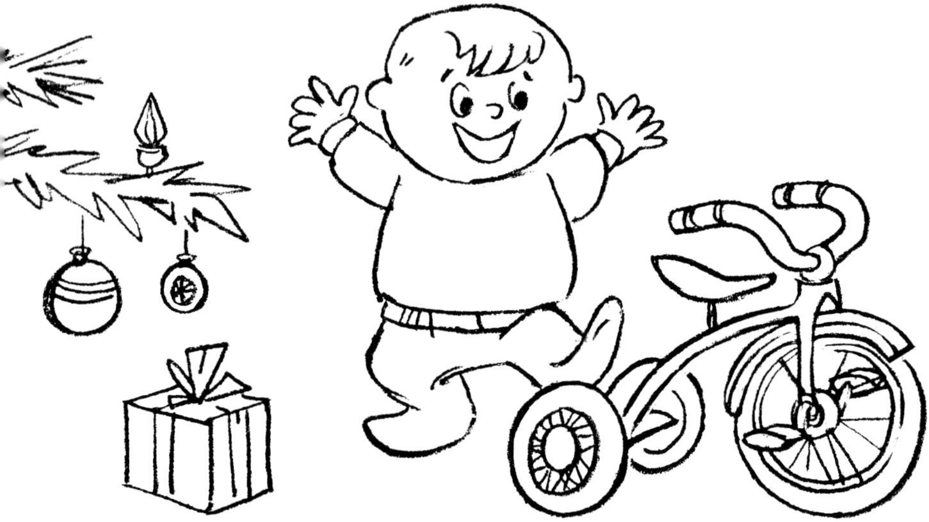

Chapter V

Indoor and Outdoor Scenes
on the same reel

One Film, Two Kinds of Light

As we've already mentioned, daylight is bluish, while tungsten light — the kind you get from your movie light — is yellowish. A different type of film is made to match each light source. As it happens, movie subjects don't fall into neat indoor-outdoor categories. A film of your picnic, for example, properly begins with mother making the sandwiches and packing the basket in the kitchen. The next scene takes you outdoors and on your way. Many movies of your family activities combine indoor and outdoor action.

Happily, there's an easy way to shoot both indoors and outdoors on one type of film: Type A. Use it indoors with movie lights. Use it outdoors with a KODAK No. 85 Filter over the lens to convert it to daylight balance. Type A film used outdoors with a filter has the same speed and uses the same exposure settings as its corresponding Daylight Type. Many movie cameras have a KODAK No. 85 Filter built right into the camera. *Every* KODAK INSTAMATIC Movie Camera has such a filter.

65

If you make an indoor movie with photoflood lamps and Daylight Type film, all of the colors will turn out much more yellowish than normal.

When Type A film is used outdoors without a filter, the results will look like this. All colors have a strong bluish cast.

Magazine Cameras

There's another way to handle the indoor-outdoor problem if you own a magazine-loading camera. Film for magazine cameras come in a lighttight metal can. It's easy to switch back and forth between Daylight Type and Type A film as the situation demands. Just be sure to jot down on each magazine the exact reading of the camera's footage meter when you remove it. Then, when you put the partially used magazine back into the camera, you'll know where to reset the footage indicator. (This isn't necessary with 16mm magazines, since the footage is indicated by the magazine itself.)

You can make movies at night on either Daylight Type or Type A film. Pictures made on Daylight Type film will have a "warmer," or more orange appearance than those shot on Type A film, but both are pleasing. With automatic cameras, the low-light pointer may indicate that you can't make movies outdoors at night. This is because the camera's meter is influenced by the large areas of darkness around the subject. Actually, any movie camera with an f2.7 lens or faster can make good movies of brightly-lit night subjects such as those shown here.

67

getting to the ZOO

Almost every movie camera owner who also chances to be a parent is at some time beset by a suspicion that he hasn't made a reel of the children for an unwholesomely long time. So he buys film and if there isn't anything special going on, no birthdays or other childhood milestones, he wonders what in the world to do with it. Often, as demonstrated here, a very satisfactory answer is to devote that film to a normal Saturday or Sunday in the life of your small fry. Getting up, eating, bathing, going to the zoo may seem prosaic stuff, but the results will turn out surprisingly captivating. Especially here is it desirable to do all of the shooting on Type A film and use a Daylight Filter over the lens outdoors. Then, wherever the kids go and whenever they go, you and your camera can go along, too.

68

I like to greet the dawn as early as the next fellow, as long as the next fellow isn't my boy, Tommy.

He can be as persistent as a tax collector until he gets his glass of orange juice . . .

. . . and he gets every bit of it.

Meanwhile, another early riser is due for a little liquid refreshment, and small Douglas . . .

. . . doesn't mind it at all.

In fact, it's the getting out that he doesn't care for, . . .

. . . but a bottle helps make him forget that.

It was much too nice out to stay indoors, so out we went . . .

. . . with mother's little helper leading the way to the park.

The drinking fountain turned out to be even better than a shower or a swimming pool.

Eventually we wandered over to the children's zoo . . .

. . . but Tommy wasn't completely sure he liked it at first.

He finally discovered, though, that these kids were just like any other kids, and began to warm up a bit.

The burro looked like a pretty friendly old cuss . . .

. . . and once I had given a feeding demonstration, . . .

. . . Tommy was all for going it solo.

We had been feeding animals so much that we finally decided we ought to start feeding boys . . .

. . . and daddies too.

But even the most avid and enthusiastic zoo-goer . . .

. . . eventually poops out.

Chapter VI

Splicing—
making big reels
from
little ones

How to Stop Torturing Family and Friends

Consider your audience. The lights are extinguished and everyone settles back to enjoy your movies. They aren't permitted to settle very far or very comfortably, though, because four minutes later (only two minutes if you have a 16mm camera using 50-foot loads) on will come the lights again while you rewind the film and thread a new roll through the projector. This spasmodic sort of performance is upsetting to the digestion, not to mention what it will do to one's temper.

You can avoid this jack-in-the-box approach—and greatly improve the level of your showmanship—with a modest gadget called a "splicer." A splicer provides an easy way of connecting several short rolls of home movies into one long, restful reel. Every 8mm projector can handle at least a 200-foot reel; every 16mm projector, at least a 400-foot reel.

Camera shops display splicers in a variety of price ranges. There are two basic kinds. One, such as the KODAK PRESSTAPE Splicer, makes dry splices by sticking the pieces of film together with thin, durable tapes. The other type "welds" two pieces of film together with a solvent that dissolves the film base.

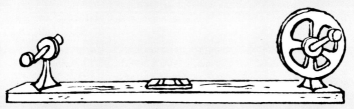

A splicing outfit made with a splicer and a pair of rewinds.

A splicing outfit using nails as axes on which the reels can turn.

In addition to the splicer, you'll need a couple of large reels onto which your small reels can be wound, and a pair of rewinds for holding the reels. You can make a rewind quite easily by anchoring your splicer in the middle of a board two or three feet long. Align the rewinds and screw one to each end of the board. You're in business.

A splicer is useful for far more than making little reels into big ones. You'll use it to remove lengths of film which are unusable because they're poorly exposed or light-struck. You'll also use it to insert titles, to rearrange scenes, and for many other tasks, all of which come under the heading of "Editing and Titling"—which happens to be the name of the chapter beginning on page 120.

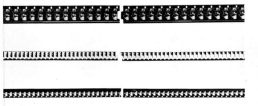

The KODAK PRESSTAPE *Universal Splicer works with 8mm, super 8, or 16mm film. It joins pieces of film together with thin, tough lengths of tape, called* KODAK PRESSTAPES.

Making a Splice with a KODAK PRESSTAPE Universal Splicer

1. Place one strip of film so that its perforations are over the pins on the left side of the splicer. (Use the top row of pins for regular 8mm and 16mm film.)

2. Place the other film strip over the pins on the right side of the splicer. The film must overlap the center line. Trim the ends of both strips with the knife in the splicer handle.

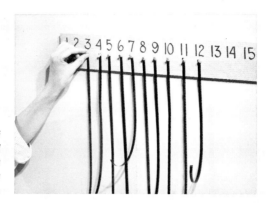

A numbered piece of cardboard or plywood provides a convenient place for hanging strips of film during editing.

3. Apply KODAK PRESSTAPE (printed side up) over the cut ends of the film by placing the tape perforations over the four fixed pins. The center line of the tape should be over the cut ends of the film.

4. After carefully removing the paper flaps, press the tape down over the pins with the punch. Turn the film over and apply another PRESSTAPE to the opposite side.

Chapter VII

Showing Your Movies

The Basic Facts of Projection

A magazine cartoon once depicted a harried moviemaker up to his kneecaps in loose film, poring manually over the remainder of his collection while his wife confided to a visitor, "I guess we'll just have to break down and buy Henry a projector." In case you've ever been in this predicament, be assured that there's nothing quite like projection for getting a good look at your movies.

The size of the image you can expect to project depends on the distance from projector to screen, the focal length of the projection lens, and the size of your film—8mm, super 8, or 16mm. The brightness of the image depends on the aperture of the projection lens, the wattage of the lamp, the distance from the screen, and the type of screen material. With some screens, your viewing angle is important, too.

Since the image size on super 8 film is bigger than on regular 8mm film, you can project them bigger and sharper than regular 8. For really big images—over 20 feet wide—you should really look to 16mm films and arc projectors. Three elements that govern image dimension are:

- ILLUMINATION PRODUCED BY PROJECTOR—*the greater the amount of light produced by a projector, the farther it will "throw" an acceptable image.*

77

- PROJECTOR-TO-SCREEN DISTANCE — *the farther from the projector to the screen, the larger the picture.*
- FOCAL LENGTH OF THE PROJECTOR LENS — *the shorter the focal length, the larger the picture at equal projector-to-screen distances; although the conventional focal lengths are one inch for 8mm projectors and two inches for 16mm, many 8mm projectors have three-quarter-inch lenses, often a desirable feature when showing films in rather small rooms. Some projectors have "zoom" projection lenses that let you vary the size of the projected image without moving the projector.*

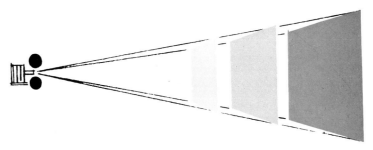

As a movie projector is moved farther from a screen, its picture will become progressively larger but also less brilliant.

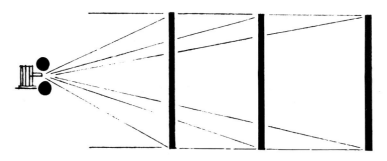

The shorter the focal length of a projection lens, the shorter the distance required for it to fill a screen with the picture.

Screens and Screenings

As you'll notice by looking at the chart of projection distances, not many rooms are big enough to let you project home movies much more than about 50 inches wide. One easy way to increase the size of the screen image in any room is to put the projector and screen in opposite corners and project diagonally. Zoom projection lenses also let you project a bigger image from a given distance than standard lenses.

PROJECTION DISTANCE FOR DESIRED SCREEN-IMAGE WIDTH

Film Size and Type	Lens Focal Length (inches)	Desired Screen-Image Width			
		40″	50″	60″	70″
		Projection Distance (Feet—to nearest ½ foot)			
8mm Motion Pictures (Regular 8)	¾	14½	18	21	26
	⅞ (22mm)	17	21	25	29
	zoom (15-25mm)	11½-19	14½-24	17-29	20-33
8mm Motion Pictures (Super 8)	1¹/₁₀ (28mm)	17½	22	26	30½
	zoom (20-32mm)	12½-20	15½-25	18½-30	21½-35
16mm Motion Pictures	1½	13	16½	20	23
	1⅝	14	17½	21	24½
	2	17½	22	26½	31
	2½	22	27½	33	38½
	3	26½	33	40	46½
	4	35½	44	53	61½

When projecting wide screen images or projecting over a long distance, make the screen area as dark as possible, and use a screen of highly reflective material.

As might be guessed, the brighter the lamp used in a projector, the brighter also will be the picture it projects. Each projector is made for use with lamps of only a certain maximum wattage. If higher-wattage lamps should be installed, the greater heat levels they create are likely to be beyond the capacities of the blower systems and heat-absorbing glass; therefore, they may endanger both the film and the projector.

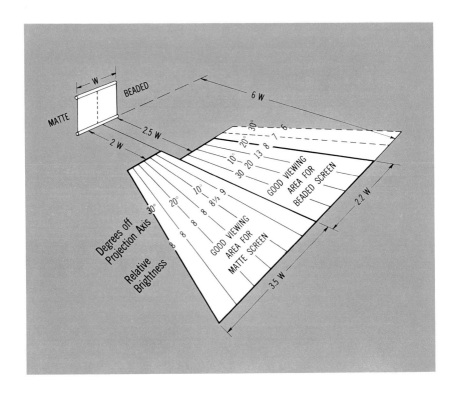

For best visibility of a movie projected onto a beaded screen, members of the audience should be seated close to the projector-screen axis. With a matte screen, the picture will not be as brilliant, but members of the audience may sit in a more spread-out pattern.

The appearance of a movie has a good deal to do with the surface on which it is projected. Beaded and aluminized screens provide a more sparkling, brilliant color image than matte screens, but they require that the viewers all be seated quite close to the line between the projector and screen.

Few makeshift screens provide nearly as good a picture as the real article, but white artist's mounting board and walls painted with flat white paint are fairly satisfactory substitutes. Colored walls inevitably degrade and tint the colors in the movie. Bed sheets, table cloths, or window shades can be used in an emergency, but, because much of the light from the projector passes through them, they cannot give you the same sort of picture as is obtained on an opaque surface.

Threading and operating procedure varies considerably from projector to projector, but the instruction booklets packaged with most of them contain clear, well illustrated instructions that should be followed closely. One recommendation applicable to all projection equipment is that, at the end of a movie, the lamp should be turned off but the motor kept operating for a few minutes. This permits the cooling fan to reduce the temperature of both the internal and external parts.

Three Suggestions For Good Shows

- Set up, thread, and focus your projector before your audience comes into the room, so that you're ready to start as soon as they're seated.
- When a reel ends and you plan to show another, don't rewind the first, but immediately thread the second. Both can be rewound later.
- Don't subject friends or acquaintances to overly long family films or movies of very restricted interest.

Part II

Chapter VIII

The mechanics of making good movies

KODAPAK Movie Cartridges

Open the camera, insert a KODAPAK Movie Cartridge, and close the camera. Start shooting. That's all there is to loading a KODAK INSTAMATIC Movie Camera. There's no motor to wind, no footage indicator to set, no threading or film handling. Remember that KODAPAK Cartridges work only in cameras that use super 8 film.

Regular 8mm Movie Film

If your 8mm camera takes conventional rolls of film, the roll that gives you 50 feet of 8mm movies actually contains 33 feet of film 16mm wide. The original width of the film is 16mm because it's designed to run through the camera twice, producing two side-by-side strips of movies. After processing, these are slit apart and spliced into a continuous strip.

Simple arithmetic indicates that a roll of 8mm film should therefore produce 66 feet of color movies. The reason it doesn't is that, there's an extra four feet of film at each end of the roll to protect the inner 25 feet from being spoiled by light during loading and unloading. This extra footage is removed after your film leaves the processing machine.

After a roll of 8mm film has run through your camera once, all of it will be on a spool marked with a reminder that only half the film has been exposed. Remove this full spool from the camera, turn it over, and reload it just as if it were a new roll of film. Turning it over is essential if each side of the film is to be exposed once. *When all else fails, read your Instruction Manual!*

Standard 16mm roll film travels through the camera only once, but it also has an extra length of film at each end of the roll for protective purposes. Never try to load regular 16mm film into an 8mm camera. It doesn't have the same kind of perforations and won't run through the camera.

8mm Magazines

When you load conventional metal magazines (*not* KODAPAK Movie Cartridges), make sure the two openings at the front of the magazine are closed before you attempt to load the camera. If film is visible, rotate the metal pin between the openings until they're both completely covered. Start the magazine with the number 1 face up. After exposing side 1, flip the magazine and expose side 2. Then have the film processed. Never remove the tape that encircles the magazine.

Exposure

A picture is taken when light reflected from a subject travels through the camera lens and strikes the film. For colors to turn out bright and natural-looking, the same amount of light must reach the film every time you push the button.

If the same amount of light were always available, we could make cameras with one lens opening and forget all about exposure. In fact, though, light varies tremendously. On a sunny day there is 16 or more times as much light striking your subject as on an overcast day. And indoors, when you're shooting with a movie light on the camera, just changing your distance from the subject from three feet to six feet reduces subject brightness by four times!

Since the light does change so often, we make cameras with adjustable openings so we can regulate the amount of light reaching the film. Modern "electric-eye" cameras automatically select the proper lens opening for almost any lighting condition. With manually adjusted cameras, you must set the correct opening yourself, but there's nothing very difficult about it. You'll find the correct openings for various lighting conditions listed

This kind of subject "fools" an automatic camera, because the bright background makes the lens close up too far to expose the foreground properly. Have your subjects all in sunlight or all in shade— not half and half.

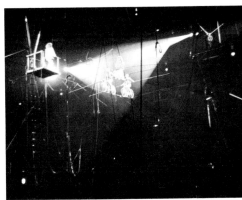

An automatic camera will indicate that you can't make movies of a subject like this. Actually, you can. The meter is influenced by the large dark area around the performers and shows a low-light warning signal. The performers themselves are really bright enough to photograph.

in the film instruction sheet, on some movie cameras, and in this chapter on page 86.

The settings used to label lens openings are called "f-numbers." These numbers show the relationship between the diameter of the lens opening and the focal length of the lens. (Focal length is the distance from a point in the lens to the film, when the lens is focused on infinity.) For example, if a lens has a focal length of 25 mm and the lens opening is 3 mm in diameter, it will be marked f8, or just plain 8. The arithmetic goes like this:

$$25/3 = f8 \text{ (approximately)}.$$

This information won't improve your movies, but it does help make sense out of a system that confuses many beginning photographers. It explains why small f-numbers are big openings, and big f-numbers represent small lens openings. In the following series, which is probably similar to the one on your camera, each number represents a lens opening that passes twice as much light as the one preceding it: 16, 11, 8, 5.6, 4, 2.8, 2 (or 1.9). One advantage of this system is that the same exposure recommendations are useful with all cameras and with lenses of any focal length.

This background is strictly for the inquisitive. All you really need to know is how to get the number that will produce well-exposed movies for you under any conditions you're likely to encounter.

Manually Adjustable Cameras

Manually adjustable cameras cost less money than automatic ones and can give the same fine movie results. The only difference is that you set the lens opening instead of a built-in mechanism. An exposure table, such as the one reproduced below, appears in the instruction sheet packaged with every roll of KODAK movie film. It shows the right lens openings to use for different kinds of lighting conditions.

Do you need an exposure meter to get good movies? Yes and no. Yes, if you frequently make movies in the shade, on overcast days, or under other unusual conditions. No, if you do most of your shooting by sunlight or with a movie light indoors.

There are dozens of different brands and types of meters. Some measure the light reflected from the subject. Others measure light falling onto the subject. No matter which type you choose, the important thing is to use it intelligently. Read its instruction book carefully and you'll be rewarded with well-exposed movies.

DAYLIGHT EXPOSURE TABLE Based on using camera speed of 16 frames per second.	Bright or Hazy Sun on Light Sand	Bright or Hazy Sun Distinct Shadows*	Cloudy Bright No Shadows	Heavy Overcast	Open Shade†
	$f/16$	Between $f/11$ and $f/16$	$f/8$	$f/5.6$	$f/5.6$
	For *average, front-lighted* subjects in daylight from two hours after sunrise to two hours before sunset.				

*For backlighted subjects, set lens at f8.

†Use a filter, such as the *Kodak* Skylight Filter (1A), to minimize the bluishness of pictures made in the open shade.

Automatic Cameras

Automatic cameras—those with built-in meters that automatically set the lens to match the lighting conditions—produce a high percentage of well-exposed movies. All you have to do is set the film-speed dial according to the table below, so the meter "knows" what kind of film you're using. (Film speeds are always printed in the film instruction sheet, too.) Putting film into a KODAK INSTAMATIC Movie Camera automatically sets the film speed.

FILM SPEEDS

For use with meters and automatic cameras marked for American Standard (ASA) Speeds or Exposure Indexes

KODAK Movie Film	Daylight	Photoflood
KODACHROME II for Daylight	25	12*
KODACHROME II, Type A	25†	40

*With KODAK No. 80B Filter
†With KODAK No. 85 Filter

NOTE: Some cameras have sky conditions marked directly on the lens settings. These may be for the old, slower KODACHROME Film, and will lead to overexposure with KODACHROME II. Be sure to check whether the markings on your camera are suitable for the current faster KODACHROME II Film.

Automatic cameras almost always produce well-exposed pictures. But there are a few situations that can "fool" them. Here are some tips for getting the most out of your automatic camera:

1. Your subjects should be all in sunlight or all in shade—not half and half.

2. When you shoot backlit subjects, shade the camera so the sun won't shine into the meter cell or camera lens.

3. Including a large area of overcast sky in the picture will cause your subjects to be underexposed. Exclude "bald" skies; they don't look good in movies anyway.

4. If the subject is very different in brightness from the background (a little girl in a white dress in front of a dark hedge, for example), move in close to the subject for best exposure.

5. Indoors, with a movie light attached to the camera, try to keep your subjects fairly close to the background.

Critical Exposure Adjustments

Frontlighting **Sidelighting** **Backlighting**

Under frontlighting, the subject faces the sun. Under sidelighting, the sun is at the side; and under backlighting, it is behind the subject. Most moviemakers are satisfied to use the setting given in exposure tables (actually the setting for frontlighting) with all three. If critical accuracy is desired, though, the lens opening should be a full stop wider for sidelighting, two stops wider for backlighting.

Light Subject **Average Subject** **Dark Subject**

A light subject consists primarily of light-colored areas, a dark subject of dark-colored or shadowed areas. Most moviemakers treat all subjects as average (nearly all are) and use the same lens setting for all subjects that are under the same kind of lighting. If critical accuracy is desired, though, the lens opening should be a half-setting smaller for a light subject, a half-setting wider for a dark subject.

Most moviemakers don't take enough close-ups. Even the least expensive, fixed-focus 8mm movie camera will let you get this close —get into the habit of moving in close to your subjects.

Viewfinding

The only feature even faintly tricky about your camera viewfinder is that you simply don't see exactly the same picture through it that the film sees through the lens. The reason? Simply because the finder is generally located about two inches above the lens. While this situation, called "parallax," may seem to present all sorts of intriguing and irritating problems, be assured that it actually causes few. It really has no practical effect on all but a very small proportion of most people's moviemaking.

The view through the finder varies from the view through the lens by inches. Only in extreme close-ups will these inches be critical.

The difference between what you see and what the lens sees is only about two inches on most cameras. No matter whether your subject is twenty-four feet away or twenty-four inches away, there will always be two inches at the top (as you view it through your finder) that, in the final movie, will be replaced by two inches' worth that is just beneath the bottom of your view. But, at twenty-four feet, those two inches are only two inches of a subject area about seven feet high and can be ignored; at twenty-four inches, though, they account for about a third of a picture area only about six inches in height, and, unless you do something corrective, you may inadvertently be cutting off and losing some important part of your intended picture.

Quite a few cameras have built-in aids to help overcome this problem. One of them is a little mark on the side and near the top of the viewfinder. For extreme close-ups, usually at three feet or less, you should line up the top of your picture with this mark rather than the actual frame of the finder. Another type

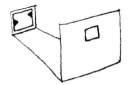 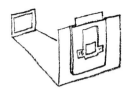 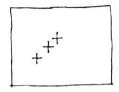

Parallax-compensating viewfinder devices may be pips against which to line up the top of the picture at close range; movable rear sights which can be raised for close-up shooting; or reticles containing off-center marks on which to center close-up scenes.

of aid is an adjustable rear sight which can be raised or lowered for different camera-to-subject distances.

The ultimate is a camera that has no parallax at all, which is exactly the case with reflex cameras that let you view right through the taking lens. The KODAK INSTAMATIC M6 Camera is one example of a talented moviemaker whose viewfinder shows the area of the scene just as it will be projected.

If your camera does not have some sort of aid for really close close-up shooting, the best thing to do about parallax is simply forget it until you wish to shoot something at three feet or less. Then merely aim the camera a little higher than the top of the subject and your film will probably turn out quite nicely.

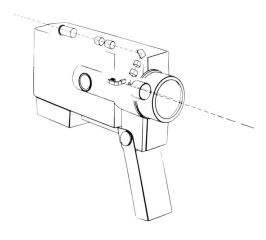

In a reflex-type movie camera, a series of optical devices direct part of the light entering the lens to the viewfinder. What you see through the viewfinder will be on the film, with no correction necessary for parallax.

Your Camera's Motor

It's a good idea, already stated and restated, to wind the spring motor of your camera after every scene. This insures that you'll never be frustrated by a "pooped-out" camera in the middle of some scintillating snapping.

With electric-drive cameras, of course, you have no winding to do. But you do have batteries to think about once in a while. You should think about them once a year, to be specific. After a year in the camera, the batteries will begin to weaken whether they've been used or not, because of the normal chemical reactions that make batteries work. You should also know that using batteries at low temperatures reduces their power and life. If you're shooting kids in the snow, ice skaters, or other cold-weather subjects, keep the camera's batteries in your pocket to keep them warm until you're actually ready to shoot. A battery that's "dead" at 0 F may be perfectly OK at 70 F.

Camera Handling

Human hands have proven capable of clamping around such diverse objects as submarine sandwiches, bowling balls, and greased pigs. They certainly, then, should have no difficulty in providing the firm fondling required by a home movie camera, in spite of its possible peculiarities of size and shape. A steady camera is an essential prerequisite of steady movies, and there's a certain arrangement of hands, wrists, and arms that fits each and every one. Chances are that your camera instruction booklet illustrates a comfortable and efficient way of holding your own particular piece of moviemaking machinery, but here are a few principles that apply almost universally.

One hand should support the camera from beneath to prevent it from jiggling up and down. In most instances, the picture button is located so that it can be operated easily by a finger of this hand. The lower arm should be vertical, and the upper arm braced close against the chest for extra support from the body.

The other hand should wrap itself around the back and one side of the camera to guard against swaying. This lower arm should also be vertical, with the upper arm tight against the side of the body. It's extremely important to do your movie snapping with arms held in close.

Don't ever swing your camera around in the casual way you might handle a garden hose. The *only* time to move the camera rapidly is when you are following some fast-moving subject. Similarly, "zoom" slowly and sparingly if your camera has a zoom lens. Too-fast or too-frequent zooms produce unsatisfactory results that are hard on the eyes. When you want to show all of some large subject in your movie, step farther back so that it will fit into your viewfinder. If this isn't possible, aim your camera at one side and then move it toward the other at an extremely slow rate. You'll notice that the professional cameramen who produce the films on display in movie theaters and for television always handle the problem in this way.

Also, never walk while you're shooting unless you're willing to accept a jarringly bumpy movie. You can, however, make some wonderfully effective films from moving cars and trains if you aim primarily at distant subjects. Results are generally best if you shoot at 24 frames per second with a wide-angle lens focused on infinity. Make sure that the window you choose has no noticeable reflections on it (since these will appear in your movies), is as clean as possible, and preferably isn't tinted. Shoot straight ahead whenever possible with the lens close to, but not in contact with, the glass.

Focusing

A lens is more than a mere window. The characteristic that distinguishes it from other slices of glassware is that it possesses the ability to focus. At some certain distance behind a lens, it will project a sharp, distinct picture of some of the things that are in front of it, and the location at which it projects this picture is the one where we want the film to be.

But, when a lens projects a picture, only objects one certain distance from that lens will be absolutely sharp. Everything in front of and behind the plane on which those objects fall will be progressively less and less sharp. The distance to this plane is called the "focus," and any lens is basically capable of being focused at almost any distance.

Fortunately, in most instances, many of the objects in front of and behind the focus distance will be so nearly as sharp as those right at the focus distance that, in looking at a picture,

With a zoom lens set at its wide-angle position, this much of the scene may be in focus.

But when you zoom out to telephoto position, depth of field decreases and only this much may be in focus.

Moral: Focus carefully when zooming in on subjects.

You can get too close! Check your camera's instruction manual to see how close you can get at various lens openings without making out-of-focus pictures.

NEAREST SHOOTING DISTANCES with Fixed-Focus 8mm Movie Cameras

Lens Settings	1.9 or 2	2.3	2.7 or 2.8	4	5.6	8	11	16
Distance in Feet	10	8½	8	6	4½	3½	2½	2

you simply cannot tell the difference. This provides, for practical purposes, a range of sharpness.

The extent of this range of sharpness depends on two factors: the actual distance for which the lens is focused and the size of the lens opening. If the lens is focused for some close-up distance, the range is rather shallow; when it is focused for a farther distance, the range becomes much greater. In addition, if the lens opening is a small one of the kind you'd use outdoors on a sunny day, the range will be greater than if the lens was focused at the exact same distance but the opening required was larger—say, f2.8, or 2.8.

The existence of this range makes possible fixed-focus movie cameras, such as some of the KODAK INSTAMATIC Movie Cameras. On these cameras, the lens focusing is preset at the factory on some intermediate distance which provides as great a range of sharpness as possible through all of the various lens openings. The far limit of sharpness at all lens openings is as far away as your eye can see (infinity); the near limits vary, depending upon the opening, and are shown in the chart on page 97.

With fixed-focus 8mm movie cameras, everything from a few feet away to as far as you can see will be in focus.

Camera Speeds

When a home movie is made at the rate of 16 frames (individual pictures) per second and then projected at this same rate, all action tends to look smooth and to duplicate the pace at which it actually occurred. If a movie is made at 32 frames per second, though, and projected at 16, all of the action appears to be taking place at a much slower rate, chiefly because it has been split up into a greater number of individual pictures. This is what makes slow motion look slow.

A camera set for slow-motion shooting at, say, 32 frames per second, simply runs the film through at a speed twice normal. Should you expose an entire roll of 8mm film at 32 frames, it will be consumed in two minutes rather than the customary four. You will, however, get four minutes of movies on your projection screen as long as the projector is operated at the standard 16 frames per second.

There's another important effect of slow-motion shooting. Each individual frame is exposed to light for a shorter period. At 32 frames it will be in front of the lens for only half as long as at 16. Unless some sort of compensating adjustment is made, a scene shot at 32 frames will turn out extremely dark due to

The more rapid the action, the more fascinating a slow-motion perusal of it will be. Slow-motion movies are an ideal means of checking your sports form. For most action, 32 frames per second will be sufficient. To check a golf swing, though, try 48 or 64.

underexposure. We can compensate for this by opening the lens to the next *larger* setting than it would be for 16 frames so that, although each frame will be exposed for only half as long, it will receive just as much light during exposure. Thus far, all of the recommended lens settings in this book have been based on shooting at 16 frames per second. Those in the table below are applicable to the other most frequently used camera speeds.

LENS SETTINGS FOR SLOW-MOTION CAMERA SPEEDS

When recommended setting at 16 Frames is:	USE SETTINGS BELOW AT			
	64 Frames	48 Frames	32 Frames	24 Frames
11	5.6	5.6—8	8	8—11
8	4	4—5.6	5.6	5.6—8
5.6	2.7 or 2.8	2.7—4 or 2.8—4	4	4—5.6
4	1.9 or 2	2—2.7 or 2—2.8	2.7 or 2.8	2.7—4 or 2.8—4
2.7 or 2.8	1.4	1.4—1.9 or 1.4—2	1.9 or 2	2—2.7 or 2—2.8

Each hyphenated setting is halfway between numbers shown.

If your camera does offer a variety of speeds, try slow motion first on sports subjects. You'll probably find that 32 frames per second will do nicely for a swimmer, diver, skier, and, in fact, any but the most rapid action. When shooting something extremely fast moving like a golfer's or ball player's swing, shift over to 48 or 64 frames. A good way to introduce a slow-motion sequence, if the action can be performed twice in a row, is to shoot it first at normal speed and then repeat it in slow motion.

Use of camera speeds slower than 16 frames per second is pretty much limited to comedy effects. Any motion photographed at 12 or 8 frames will be speeded up and will appear quite choppy, in the style of the Keystone Cops.

Chapter IX

Making movies more interesting

The Camera Tells the Story

In most cinema palaces, the popcorn vendor probably excites more conversation than the cameraman who photographed the movie. The patrons of movie theatres have come to expect that the camera will be in the right place at the right time to help the actors, directors, and writers get on with the story.

Of course, a professional cameraman does have some great advantages, not the least being that whenever anything goes other than the way it should, he has a second chance. So if Slimy McSweeney, the menace, happens accidentally to clobber the Abilene Kid in the climactic fisticuffs, they can be shot all over again.

But this involves other people's mistakes and doesn't bear on home moviemaking in which you generally take activity the way it comes. The important fact about the professional is that he tries to photograph each bit of the action in a way that will help advance the story and help the audience appreciate the comedy or drama of that story, such as it is.

In home movies, though, too often the interesting things that go on in front of the lens are obscured or lessened in impact simply because the camera is handled in a casual, almost careless way. There are three basic means by which to avoid this: variation of scene length, shifts in subject distance, and continuity.

None of these involve rigid, immutable rules. All come pretty naturally, and the more that you use them and see the results on your screen, the better moviemaker you'll become. When you begin trying them out, you'll find, perhaps to your surprise, that it really is just about as easy to shoot a good home movie as a so-so one.

Subject Distance

Before storming into a full-scale discussion of camera-to-subject distances, it probably would be advisable to make a token bow to clarity and re-define the three bits of photographic jargon most constantly exercised in explorations of this subject.

CLOSE-UP—In movies, this is a shot made about 6 feet or less from the subject. At 6 feet, with a lens of normal focal length (12 mm or 13 mm for 8mm shooting, 25 mm for 16mm cameras), most cameras will take in head and shoulders of an adult.

MEDIUM-DISTANCE SHOT—Anything snapped from 25 feet or less but not as close as 6 feet, is a "medium shot." At 25 feet, your camera covers a top-to-bottom dimension of about 6 feet.

LONG-DISTANCE SHOT—A scene of any subject farther away than 25 feet is a long shot.

All of these are scaled to the photographing of people. A close-up of the Statue of Liberty might be made from much farther away than 6 feet. The definitions are designed to fit like a stretch sock rather than a kid glove. Particularly under "medium-distance shot" is there a vast amount of latitude, and the category probably could be subdivided into "close-medium," "medium-medium," and "long-medium," but, if this were done, the chapter would begin to look more like an exercise in handling a yardstick than a collection of helpful hints on the relatively free-style pastime of making home movies.

One of the simplest things you can do that will effect the greatest improvement in your movies is to stock them amply with close-ups. At least one scene in every three or four should be a close-up. With a movie camera, close-up shooting is especially easy because, for a head-and-shoulders shot, you can be as far as 6 feet away, a distance from which you aren't too likely to give your subject twinges of self-consciousness. For the same kind of shot with a still camera, you'd have to be nearer than 3 feet.

A good formula, very often, is to start some movie sequence with a long shot to establish location, follow with a medium shot to show what's going on, and then move in for a close-up or two to pinpoint action. This can't be applied to every situation, but it does fit a great many.

CLOSE-UP: *This is usually made from 6 feet or nearer, includes head and shoulders of a person.* MEDIUM-DISTANCE SHOT: *This can be made at a distance of from 6 to 25 feet, can show an adult in standing position.* LONG-DISTANCE SHOT: *This is made at a shooting distance of more than 25 feet.*

Actually, the best distance from which to shoot a scene is the closest distance that provides a complete view of whatever is occurring. When shooting a certain activity, this distance will frequently change, and so should your camera position.

This sounds like nothing but common sense. But, the more movies you make, the more evident it will become that the best are those in which you apply such rules of common sense by varying camera-to-subject distance, spicing your shooting with close-ups, and shooting each slice of activity from the nearest distance which permits you to include all important elements.

101

Continuity

"Continuity" uses five syllables to express what "story" does in two. Whenever a series of scenes has some sort of basic unity, usually because it shows the progress of a certain activity, and if the scenes appear in logical sequence, you have a natural story and natural continuity.

The alternative is a collection of moving snapshots with nothing linking them but the film itself. Once the owner of a movie camera finds that the original novelty of just being able to make pictures that *move* has begun to pall, such snapshot reels are likely to start seeming rather dull and boring.

If, when your mind juggles together the words "movie" and "continuity," visions appear of elaborate scenarios, Cecil B. DeMille in puttees, and a cast of thousands, sit down, relax, and regroup your thoughts. For the kind of home movie continuity in which most people are interested, no rehearsals and no heavy planning are needed. Occasionally, though, a social director's knack of keeping things moving comes in handy.

In many instances, all the action needed for a good film will be entirely impromptu. In others, it may be necessary to have some scenes acted out specially, either because they add something that makes the movie more interesting or to repeat a happening that occurred, perhaps, when you were too far away or not in a position to shoot. Often, too, continuity can be enhanced by removing certain sections of film entirely or even by rearranging the order of some scenes. The why's and how's of this are covered in the chapter on editing which begins on page 120.

Although the lily can sometimes be gilded by having certain scenes acted out or by editing, the foundation of a good home movie is still natural activity. If you're intent on making your films as interesting as possible, you've got to start with more than a mere decision to shoot some movies, period. Either you must wait for some interesting activity to start spontaneously or take a hand in starting it yourself.

There are several common tricks you can use to help promote a feeling of smooth continuity in your movies. For example, whenever the setting is going to change from indoors to outdoors or vice versa, end one scene with the subject going through a door and then, when you begin the next one in the new setting, it will tend to make much more sense. If the setting is going to change between two scenes but will remain indoors or outdoors, merely let the subject walk right out of the picture area in one setting and, when you start the next scene, have the subject walk into the picture area, preferably from a different angle, although the same direction.

Basically, though, nearly all of the continuity you will ever need is built right into the activities that lend themselves to good home movies. It's just a matter of confining your moviemaking to these activities and occasionally adding to the normal proceedings a few ideas that will make the story more interesting.

Scene Length

While it's easy enough to report that the average home movie scene should run about 10 seconds in length, it isn't quite so easy to dispel the sinister overtones trailing along behind.

SINISTER OVERTONE A: That there's a faint aroma of the stopwatch in this moviemaking business. Actually, not so. Anyone playing around with a movie camera has enough on his mind while merely attending to correct exposure and keeping up with his subject to preclude any faint possibility that he might also do a bit of timekeeping on the side. Anyway, it just isn't necessary.

SINISTER OVERTONE B: That, since the average scene should last for about 10 seconds, all scenes should be 10 seconds long. Emphatically, not so. Aside from the outright monotony of it, this would be rather like buying a half dozen size 7 dungarees for a family of six children and then altering the pants to each child's individual requirements.

An individual movie scene should be exactly as long as it needs to be. If the person or persons you are photographing are doing something interesting, keep your finger on the camera button until they cease to be interesting or until your shooting distance ceases to be the best one. If the action demands a closer shot or a farther one, stop shooting and shift position.

104

CONTINUITY AT WORK

This story tells itself. When the activity shifts from a lesson to story-reading or then to snack time, you see what's going on. Notice how much the close-ups contribute. The pictures were made on KODAK TRI-X *Film, which permits owners of 16mm cameras to shoot indoor movies without a light bar.*

Unfortunately, this is rather like telling a new bride how to compound a tricky pie filling entirely in terms of bits and pinches, when she's still not even certain how many teaspoonfuls make a tablespoon. About the only means of offering quantitative help is to say that very, very few scenes should ever be any briefer than 5 seconds; and equally few, any longer than 15. A film having lots of short scenes tends to seem spasmodic and jerky, while one in which the scenes are all long will drag.

The most entertaining movie is usually one in which there's considerable variety in scene length, with short scenes following long scenes, and with each individual scene lasting just long enough to contribute its special piece of action. Generally, there's enough natural variety in the length of time that chunks of activity last to provide this automatically.

You and your movie camera might, on some bright day, be off on a hike with a group of Campfire Girls who were just about to build, of all things, a campfire. The girls start bringing wood to some chosen location and you stand back with your camera to shoot this. After about 10 or 12 seconds, this parade of branch and stick bearers just starts to seem pretty repetitive, so you stop. You might, then, come in closer and shoot some footage of the girl who's arranging the fuel in regulation campfire style, probably for not more than 8 or 10 seconds because that's all it requires to show quite well what she's up to. If you want a close-up of her applying flaming match to kindling, chances are that this little scene wouldn't last more than 5 seconds. The action is an extremely brief one, and that's all you'd need to capture it satisfactorily.

Occasionally, a few very brief scenes can be used advantageously to get a feeling of fast pace in certain sorts of movies. If you were making a film of two small boys poking away at each other with boxing gloves, a linking of brief close-ups of gloves making contact with chins, faces, and noses would make the action seem even more furious than it probably was.

Some beginners have a tendency to shoot extremely short scenes, perhaps in an attempt to get more "mileage" from a roll of film. It's a false economy. A series of such short scenes look very choppy on the screen. Your goal should always be to mix long, short, and medium scene lengths for variety and interest.

What's happening determines to a great degree the length of each scene. The initial one here might be fairly long and the second short or vice versa, just so they demonstrate that the boy is building a jump for his Flying Saucer. The third scene could be of medium length, but number four (which starts where the fourth picture does and ends at the fifth) must last as long as the action. For comic effect, the last scene would be a rather brief one.

Chapter X

Effects with Wide-Angle, Telephoto, and Zoom Lenses

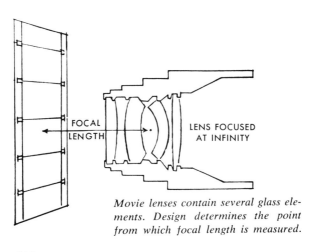

Movie lenses contain several glass elements. Design determines the point from which focal length is measured.

Focal Length

Through the wizardry of optics, you and your camera can remain in one position while your lenses whisk you close to distant action or shift you farther away from subjects so big or so close that they don't fit into the viewfinder.

With a wide-angle lens on your camera, everything in your picture will look smaller and farther away than with the normal lens, your camera will "see" a wider angle of view, and you will be able to get more in the picture from a given spot.

Telephoto lenses, on the other hand, make your subjects look bigger and closer to the camera than the normal lens does. They let you "move in" on your subject without actually changing your shooting position. Telephoto lenses also magnify camera movement. Movies made through a telephoto lens will look very bouncy if you don't hold the camera steady.

There are several ways to enjoy the advantages of wide-angle and telephoto shooting, depending on what kind of camera you have. They all depend on changing the focal length of the lens. You don't really need to understand focal length to make good movies, but it will help you predict your results.

Focal length is the distance from a point in the lens to the film, when the camera is focused on infinity. Usually it's marked, either in inches or millimeters, somewhere on the lens mount. "Normal" focal length for an 8mm or super 8 camera is 12 mm or 13 mm. Any focal length greater than that produces telephoto pictures. Any focal length shorter than that produces wide-angle pictures.

A zoom lens lets you "move in" on the subjects you see without actually changing your own shooting position.

With the zoom lens in its wide-angle position, the scene might look like this.

Without moving, you can slowly zoom your lens to its "normal" position for a view like this.

Continue zooming to the telephoto position for this view. Always zoom slowly and sparingly.

Zoom Lenses

The most modern, flexible, and convenient way to enjoy the advantages of different focal lengths is with a zoom lens. A zoom lens is a single lens whose focal length can be varied continuously between wide-angle, regular, and telephoto positions. In other words, a zoom lens can do the work of several lenses of different focal lengths and also permit you to zoom in close or "back away" while you're filming.

The novelty of a zoom lens is almost irresistible. People with zoom lenses often zoom in and out on every scene simply because the lens lets them do it. This is sort of like tooling down to the corner drugstore at 120 miles an hour because you happen to own a powerful sports car. It may be fun, but the results can be disastrous. Here are some tips on using a zoom lens properly.

First, zoom sparingly. Two or three times a roll is plenty. Zoom slowly. Zooming in and out too fast is just as bad as panning too fast. And for heaven's sake, never commit the ultimate moviemaking sin of panning *and* zooming at the same time.

Here's another important point about zoom lenses. When they're in their telephoto position, zoom lenses have less depth of field than normal or wide-angle lenses. Depth of field is the distance in front of and behind your subject that will be in sharp focus. *Focus carefully when zooming in on a subject.* If you don't, you're likely to zoom the subject right out of focus as your lens reaches its telephoto position.

The real beauty of a zoom lens is that it provides a quick, easy way of letting you fill the viewfinder with a particular subject. As a rule, *before* you start shooting, find the lens position that gives the best framing.

Basically, a zoom lens can be considered a replacement for a turret camera or for separate, interchangeable lenses. It can do the same things interchangeable lenses can do, plus more. And it makes a less bulky package. In the sections that follow, there are tips for using wide-angle and telephoto lenses. Everything that's said about these also applies to zoom lenses when they're set at their wide-angle or telephoto positions.

111

Whether you'd like to show one solitary little bird or a screen full of them, there's a movie lens available that will make the job easier. A telephoto lens or lens converter is ideal for photographing small subjects that can't be too closely approached on foot.

112

To appreciate fully what a super-telephoto lens (one of 38mm or greater focal length for 8mm shooting, 63mm or greater for 16mm) can do, you must see actual movies made with one. At an exciting corrida you may be far up in the grandstand, but a super-telephoto puts your camera right behind the matador's shoulder.

A telephoto lens offers a special dividend when used for movies of nature subjects. It not only provides frame-filling close-ups but also creates an attractively out-of-focus background.

Nothing can keep you more effectively away from a prospective movie subject than bars. But a telephoto lens spans distance that you can't, makes it possible to shoot excellent zoo films.

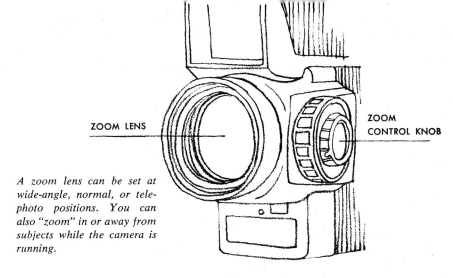

ZOOM LENS

ZOOM CONTROL KNOB

A zoom lens can be set at wide-angle, normal, or telephoto positions. You can also "zoom" in or away from subjects while the camera is running.

How and When to Use a Telephoto

A telephoto lens is invaluable for making movies of subjects you can't get as close to as you might wish — spectator sports, birds and animals, planes and trains. It will help you capture wonderfully natural childhood activity, since you can shoot from far enough away so your quarry won't guess there's a camera anywhere in the vicinity.

With telephoto lenses of more than about three times the focal length of your camera's normal lens, it's rather difficult to get a really steady picture unless you use a tripod. Slight camera movement usually isn't evident in movies made with lenses of normal focal length but a telephoto will magnify it to the same degree as it magnifies the size of objects. Modern tripods are

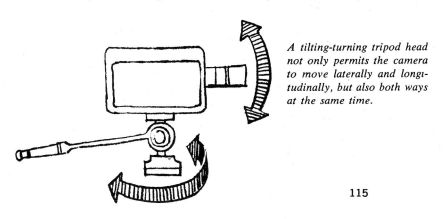

A tilting-turning tripod head not only permits the camera to move laterally and longitudinally, but also both ways at the same time.

115

lightweight and can be condensed into pocket-sized packages. For movie shooting, it's important to have one with a tilting-turning head device so that you can move your camera smoothly as you follow your subject. A tripod of this type will cost approximately twenty dollars.

In addition, telephoto lenses have a narrower range of sharp focus than lenses of normal focal length. Distance from camera to subject should be estimated with considerable care, especially for fairly close scenes. When extreme close-ups are photographed with a telephoto lens, it's essential to make an actual measurement.

Shooting with a Wide-Angle Lens

A wide-angle lens expands the indoors. With a lens of only normal focal length you often discover that you can't get as much area into your scenes as you'd like. Either it's because a wall stops you from backing up any farther or because, when you're able to back up far enough, your photofloods are so far from the subject that you can't get a satisfactory exposure.

But, with a wide-angle lens or lens converter you can beat both problems. If you're back-to-wall and still don't have enough distance between you and your subject, a 9mm wide-angle lens on your 8mm camera has the effect of stretching that range by half-again more than it is. If you find that it takes a camera-to-subject distance of 20 feet to get subjects full length, but that your two-lamp light bar doesn't provide enough illumination, a wide-angle lens will include just as much area at 14 feet, from where the lamps do provide enough.

A wide-angle lens is also helpful outdoors for squeezing a large building or natural wonder into a movie frame. It also does a better job than the lens of normal focal length when you shoot movies through the windshield of a moving vehicle.

One of the greatest advantages of having both wide-angle and telephoto lenses at your command is the marvelous variety they can provide for shooting films of sports events, outdoor entertainments, graduation ceremonies, or other situations when your own location is fixed. By switching from one lens to the other, your film will have a pleasant variety where it might otherwise seem dull and monotonous.

116

Wide-angle lenses are especially useful indoors, and in cramped quarters where you can't get back very far from the subject. Lenses on movie cameras have a narrower acceptance angle than lenses on still cameras. A wide-angle lens on a movie camera takes in less of the scene than the standard lens on most still cameras.

117

With a wide-angle lens you can cram a large area onto the film even when, as in a boat, you aren't able to move back any farther (top). It also helps exaggerate distance for effect (middle) and gives you nearly full-length views of people in rather small rooms.

Size and scope are a wide-angle lens' bread and butter. So many vast natural and man-made wonders would appear considerably less breathtaking than they are unless shown complete and whole in the movies shot of them. A wide-angle lens does this superlatively.

Chapter XI

Editing and Titling

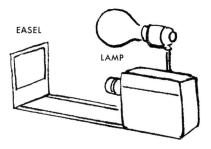

EASEL

LAMP

A movie titler presents your imagination with a willing sparring partner. Maps, photographs, a typewriter, printed illustrations, stick-on letters, and colored paper all become potential titling tools.

A complete editing outfit permits you to check your movie footage carefully yet easily, mark it for any subsequent cutting, make good solid splices, and wind it onto a single reel.

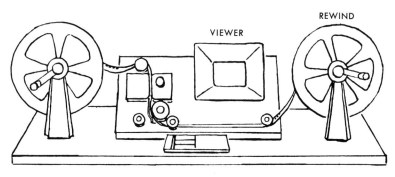

REWIND

VIEWER

SPLICER

Equipment for Editing and Titling

You can accomplish a primitive form of editing with nothing more than the splicing board mentioned in Chapter VI. For speed and convenience, you'll do better with a commercially-made unit which includes a splicer, a pair of rewinds, and possibly even a small preview screen. Your photo dealer will show you the various kinds of equipment available to make your editing easier.

You can make many of your titles without any special equipment by photographing signs, historical markers, and other "natural" titles you encounter in your travels. You can even write titles in the wet sand of a beach or in the snow.

Commercially-made titlers are available for a number of movie cameras. They offer convenience and flexibility in making a variety of titles. Again, your photo dealer will show you what's available.

No matter what kind of equipment you own, buy, or build, the important thing is to realize its extreme usefulness in making your movies more fun to see. Changing the sequence of scenes, shortening scenes, or taking some scenes out altogether can improve almost any length of movie film ever shot. Hollywood's top professionals wouldn't dream of trying to create a film without heavy reliance on film editors. Chances are you're not better at moviemaking than they are.

Just having editing equipment on your shelf doesn't make your movies any better. You have to use it. Frankly, most people don't bother—and their pictures show it. There's nothing hard about making titles or editing home movies. Doing them well is what this chapter is all about.

Project your film and decide what order you want the scenes in. Cut the scenes apart and hang on numbered push-pins as shown. Then reassemble your film in the right order.

It's easy to make a home-made movie titler from two pieces of wood. A movie light provides an easy way of getting enough illumination.

BUD and SELF with AFRICAN SHIELD

M

AN EXAMPLE OF EDITING
*This is a scene card for editing a movie. The heading at the top
identifies the scene. The "M" indicates it is a medium-distance scene.
The remaining space would contain any corrective notes.*

*Imagine that each of the pictures here is a complete scene on a
movie reel returned to you from the processing laboratory. The
adjoining comments would be those written on your scene cards.
To see the result of this editing, turn to pages 128 and 130.*

BIT TOO LONG—
CUT OUT SOME OF
CONCLUDING FOOTAGE

TOO UNDEREXPOSED—
CHOP OUT ENTIRELY

OK

CUT SOME EARLY
FOOTAGE SO TRAIN
EMERGES FROM TUNNEL
AS SCENE BEGINS

MOVE FARTHER FRONT
SO IT COMES <u>BEFORE</u>
FIRST VIEW OF TRAIN
AND BECOMES TITLE

OK

UNEXPOSED FILM FROM
TURNING REEL OVER FOR
SECOND RUN THROUGH
CAMERA — CHOP OUT

CUT OUT PART AT END
WHEN BUD LOOKS
AT CAMERA

CAMERA MOVED —
CHOP OUT ENTIRELY

OK

The Technique of Editing

The difference between mere splicing and editing is about the same as that between painting a house and painting a picture. Although the tools are pretty much the same, the approach to one is much more creative and sophisticated than to the other.

Editing is a cosmetic kind of treatment for home movies. Like any cosmetic, it can't transform basically poor original material into something artful and lovely. Even the wonders of photography aren't capable of turning the sow's-ear-to-silk-purse trick. But, with predominantly good original footage, it can perform a remarkable polishing job.

In the editing process, long scenes can be shortened to enhance the pace of the movie. Poorly focused, badly exposed, uninteresting, or irrelevant footage can be removed. Scenes can be rearranged in different order if the new order yields better continuity or a more interesting result. It's even possible to combine scenes made at different times and on different reels. Humorous footage can be chopped into short sections and inserted at various places in the movie to provide a running gag. And, when specially made titles are also added during editing, the result, depending upon the quality of the original reels and the imagination of the editor, can be pretty nearly the acme of home moviemaking.

Of course, a tremendous amount of editing can be done in the camera if you photograph activities in their normal sequence, include natural titles whenever possible, strive to avoid exposure and focusing errors, and work for natural continuity. The greater your success in doing these things, the more value you get from your investment in film. But if 90 percent of a reel is so good that you wouldn't want to alter it in any way (and 90 percent is an unusually high batting average), the additional ten percent might be so glaring to an audience of family and friends that it would overshadow the quality of the larger portion. It's hardly an exaggeration to say that almost every reel returned from a processing laboratory can become a better movie through some editing.

The process of editing is fun. It has much of the appeal for adults that pasting pictures into a scrapbook has for kids. In fact, the similarity is great even though the editing materials are somewhat more complex.

Some editing can be done almost like mental arithmetic. It merely involves running a reel of film through your editor, snipping out occasional dull or poorly photographed sections, rearranging one or two scenes, and adding a title at the beginning. In this sort of once-over-lightly editing, you can carry all the necessary ideas in your head and need never commit the intended organization of your movie to writing.

But full-scale editing requires more planning. To start, place yourself in a chair and the chair within arm's length of your projector. Make sure that there's a package of small file cards on the table in front of you and a pencil at hand.

Start the projector and make out a card for each individual scene by jotting down a few identifying words at the top of the card. If you have a preponderance of brief scenes, you may have to run the reel through more than once.

After you have made all the scene cards, project the film again. This time, make editing analysis notes on the cards. Indicate whether the scene is primarily a long-distance, medium-distance, or close-up one. If its content is exactly as you want it, mark a check on the card. If the scene is too long or if part of it has areas of fog from incorrect loading or if portions are out of focus or if exposure is poor or for any other reason it should be cut out, note that down, too. Before long you'll probably develop a handy code.

Once you've finished this analysis, add scene cards for any scenes on other reels of film that logically belong with those on the reel you've just looked at. Often scenes made at different times fit together quite neatly. Doing this isn't cheating. The entire idea of editing, after all, is to assemble an interesting movie, not necessarily a chronologically exact record.

If you're putting together a vacation film, you might have three, four, or even more sets of scene cards from as many individual reels shot during the course of your travels. You might also have made some special titles on a separate reel. Add the cards for all of these together into one big stack.

Now arrange the cards in the order you think most interesting. As you do this, remember that you'll be doing some cutting, as indicated by the comments on the cards. This phase of editing is the one in which you should drop out the cards representing scenes either too weak photographically or too irrelevant for your final movie.

In shuffling these cards, you needn't be guided strictly by the chronological order in which events really occurred. If some other order seems reasonable and more interesting, use it. On a vacation trip, you might have spent the first and second days sightseeing and the third day swimming. Just for variety, it probably would be better to insert the swimming sequences between the two groups of scenic material.

As you arrange and rearrange your scene cards, keep striving for natural continuity and check your markings of subject distance so you don't, inadvertently, link together extensive chains of either all long-distance scenes or close-ups. When you finally get the order that appeals to you most, consider whether any special titles might be advantageous in certain spots. Returning to the example of a vacation film, if you were showing a trip during which you visited two or three national parks and stayed at a couple of memorable lodges, it might be worthwhile to have a title for each park and lodge to precede the scenes showing them.

Once you have *all* your film at hand, both original footage and special titles, and all of your scene cards representing them, number the cards consecutively from the top of the pile down. At this point you'll find it especially handy to have a unique piece of editing equipment, strictly homemade. Get one or two metal wastepaper baskets. Out of scraps, make a wooden "T," the upright two to three feet high and the crossbar about as wide as the wastebasket. Nail a row of ordinary brads into the crossbar with a quarter-inch of each sticking out. If you shoot 8mm film, place the brads about a half-inch apart. Number the brads consecutively from left to right. If you make two of these gadgets, and it's an especially good idea to have two for 16mm editing, begin numbering the brads on the second where you left off with those on the first. Then bolt each upright to the back of a wastepaper basket.

Next, run through the editor each reel of film containing scenes for your movie. Place a nick at the beginning and end of every scene you plan to use and cut the scenes apart at the nick

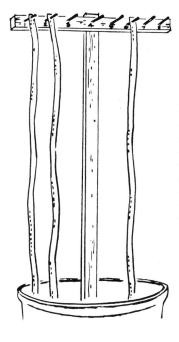

A film editing "T" is simply what it appears to be, a wooden "T" fastened to a wastepaper basket. Small brads should be nailed into the horizontal member and spaced far enough apart so that strips of film can be hung from them. It's helpful if the brads are numbered consecutively.

marks. If two or more scenes follow each other on both the original reels and the cards, however, there's no need to cut them apart. As you remove each scene, hang it by its top perforation from the brad having the same number as its card. It's advisable to wear a pair of inexpensive white cotton gloves while you are handling the film. When several scenes are connected together, hang them from the number of the first scene on the strip, but leave vacant the brads marked with the numbers of the others. The tails of the film can hang down into the basket.

When this is done, the scenes will be in the same order as their cards. Simply edit the individual lengths of film as indicated by your comments on the cards and, once you've finished this, splice them together, starting at number one. Be careful, though, not to cinch the film tight on its reel, since this can scratch it severely.

This is a home movie story that has been edited. How the editing was performed on a portion of it is shown on pages 122 and 123. Also, though, it is an example of the manner in which the presence of just a few titles can enhance any home movie. In this instance we have a "manufactured" title at the very beginning and several natural titles farther along. All of these titles fall into place quite unobtrusively and, in a sense, assume the role performed in a book by chapter headings. They not only break up the overall story into smaller, more digestible chunks, but also, and perhaps even more important, they serve to introduce new settings and new activities. Note how, in this as in all of the other complete movie stories shown earlier in the book, the frequent use of attractive close-ups makes a valuable contribution.

The Santa Fe and Disneyland R.R. must be one of the busiest lines in the world, so . . .

. . . when our train chugged into the old-fashioned terminal . . .

. . . we didn't waste any time in getting aboard one of the coaches.

It brought us quickly from the everyday world into the amazing and magical world of Disneyland.

It seemed like a good idea to get properly togged out . . .

. . . so we looked into the head-gear situation. It was an especially hard choice for Bud . . .

. . . and he finally ended up by wheedling three out of me.

Nearby we ran into a display of shields and he'd have liked a couple of them, too.

Although we'd done a little railroading already, we didn't want to miss . . .

Even the most enthusiastic sight-seers need some sustenance . . .

. . . a ride behind Casey Jones and his steam calliope.

. . . and Bud tackled a hamburger just about as big as the boy.

The route was really tremendous, complete with tunnel "carved" out of solid rock.

Karen did all right, too.

The kids decided that they'd been earthbound long enough, so . . .

. . . they chose to climb aboard an airborne elephant.

There's Karen. She's wondering whether it mightn't have been a good idea to take a parachute.

A little later on we found an old-time ice cream cart.

Naturally, this had considerable attraction to the small fry.

And, as you can guess, they were less than overjoyed when we had to head for home.

Ways, Means, and Ideas for Titling

For a moment, transplant yourself from behind the projector out into one of your home-movie audiences. Let's say that the screen is bustling with scenes of the kids at the zoo. You can see them clambering up onto a fence and craning for a better view. Then there's a close-up of their delighted faces, then the aquatic gymnastics of the sea lions who are entertaining them, then Mom in the midst of a kaleidoscope of pansies.

The effect is a lot like shifting suddenly from a forward gear into reverse. If the screech isn't aural, it's certainly mental. You can explain the abrupt transition by mentioning aloud that, after touring the zoo, you walked over to the botanical gardens, but this still doesn't eliminate the basic awkwardness.

The neatest means of handling a situation like this would simply have been to aim the camera at the sign identifying the gardens and shoot about five seconds' worth of film before making any other scenes there. This would have created a title, and titles are the best introductions and transitions. They need be no more complex than this one.

Fortunately for home moviemakers, the landscape is liberally dotted with prospective title material erected by states, municipalities, park commissions, historical societies, highway departments, and commercial enterprises. Ships' life preservers are good titles. So are the names painted on airliners. To shoot this kind of title, just get as close as your camera and the situation will permit and keep the button pressed down for about twice as long as is needed to read the printing slowly. No title, however, should ever be briefer than about five seconds.

Should you lack a ready-made title, ingenuity can often move mountains. A movie tour of a garden might be introduced by an over-the-shoulder view of some seed packets being held by the gardener. Indoors, you'll discover that items as simple as a child's blackboard, alphabet blocks, or anagram letters can be used advantageously. If you're planning to shoot some local festival, a newspaper with a banner headline announcing it makes a fine title. A birthday cake, all by itself, is a wonderful title, one that can have a little extra action added by having someone outside the picture area blow out the candles while you're shooting.

Occasionally, you can even shoot a special introduction to the title, itself. For a family fishing expedition you might make a brief scene of the youngest fisherman in your brood proudly holding a large fish while Dad, displaying something about the size of a runt sardine, glowers. In editing, this scene could be placed just before the highway marker giving the name of the lake. To precede some first films of a newborn baby, you might shoot some male feet pacing back and forth across the floor until, suddenly, they stop and a pair of female feet in white shoes appears in the picture. Then the actual title, an open box of cigars with a small sign giving vital statistics pinned to it, could follow.

There's nothing at all tricky about this sort of titling. These are ordinary movie scenes which can be shot at any time and later spliced into another reel. The important ingredient is imagination.

With titling equipment designed for photographing typewritten title copy, you can transform a magazine illustration, a color snapshot, a section from a map, a picture postcard, or even part of a travel folder into a colorful title. Some of these will probably be complete in themselves and can go into the titler as is. Others can be used as backgrounds on which the text is typed or lettered.

The text portion of any title should be kept as brief as possible, no longer than eight to ten words. One of the most readily available and versatile instruments for preparing text is a typewriter, since it can print on wallpaper, poster paper, the light areas of a photographic print, and numerous other surfaces. For dark, sharp titles, the typewriter's ribbon should be new or nearly new.

Another easy way of engineering text material is via the ceramic and wooden letters sold in sets by many photo shops. These can be fastened to a background card or picture with double-coated cellophane tape.

Should you own any skill with pen or brush, it can be exercised profitably in the production of home movie titles. Start with a rectangle of cardboard or colored paper, just so long as it's the size required for your titler, and let your ingenuity run unchecked. If it's a challenge to you to draw a reasonably

TITLES UNLIMITED

Just about everywhere that you and your movie camera go there are natural titles on hand, free for the taking. Sometimes they'll be quite conventional, such as road signs or historical markers; sometimes, though, they may be as unique and interesting as the place they describe. The "Bears and Barbed Wire" sign is an excellent example. Here is a small sampler of natural titles merely to demonstrate the enormous variety of title material available.

134

135

LIFE IN THE AQUARIUM

With a titler, a small sheet of clear plastic material, and some plastic letters you can create live titles like this one quite easily.

straight line, you may find it entirely within your artistic capabilities to make wonderfully colorful titles with scissors and paste. First, cut a rectangle of colored paper of the size used by your titler. This will be the background. Then merely cut some simple shapes out of other colors to form either a design or a simple picture, paste them on the background, type the text material, and shoot.

Since some commercially made titlers can also be used for ultra close-up moviemaking, this presents some additional titling possibilities. You might, for instance, cut a sheet of clear rigid plastic to the dimensions of your titler easel and place a few words on it, either by inking them in or with movable letters. This can then be mounted in the titler and some flowers, a kitten's face, a mounted butterfly, or some fish swimming in an aquarium placed directly behind it. When this sort of titling is done, it's especially important for the titler to be held steady.

Actually, the greatest pitfall of titling is that, once you start doing it, the process may become so engrossing that you'll tend to overload your films with title material. Titles should be employed only to introduce movies and to explain things about them that aren't self-apparent. The movie itself should still be the chief attraction.

Running Gags and "Orphaned" Film

Editing and titling, then, are post-shooting methods of smoothing out your movies, making them more intelligible, enhancing their continuity. There aren't any strict rules for good editing or good titling, only methods. Just as everyone will film a certain event in a different way, everyone edits and titles to the tune of his own taste, patience, and capabilities.

Although most editing and titling is done to improve some sort of natural story that already exists on one or more reels of film, both can be used to accomplish even more.

They can, for example, furnish a liberal helping of humor. You might be filming a Saturday's activities around the house. Perhaps someone has acquired a new car, and his tender loving care of it has become something of a family joke. If you can catch this person out washing or polishing his pride-and-joy, shoot one extremely long scene of his labor of love. Then, instead of using the film all together, insert brief chunks of it in four or five different breaks between sequences entirely unrelated to it. You might precede each with a title like, "Meanwhile, back at the driveway . . ." This is called a "running gag," and there are endless variations of the technique. Mac Sennett and his contemporaries used them hilariously, and time hasn't dulled their potentialities.

Editing also permits the linking of short "orphaned" sequences that, while interesting in themselves, don't really fit into an extensive movie story. Any pair of parents who make movies of their small fry is likely to have a good deal of this sort of footage languishing around. You can make marvelous growing-up reels of children with such film by merely arranging a collection of scenes in chronological order so that, over a period of four or five minutes, you'll be able to watch a son or daughter progress from a newborn infant through all the fascinating stages of childhood. In this sort of movie, only an introductory title is essential. The movie tells its own story.

When an especially good humor and titling mood seize you simultaneously, you can often get quite funny results out of other "orphaned" film by editing it onto a comic newsreel. A title like "Great medical discovery announced" might precede a few scenes of the kids playing doctor. "New production records set" might introduce your cat or dog surrounded by a large and bustling litter. "Opportunities for computing machines" might present some sequences of a golfer having a difficult time getting out of a sandtrap. This sort of material can be linked together until you run out of film or out of bright ideas.

DOING IT YOURSELF

Homemade "manufactured" movie titles needn't be just letters lined up against a colored background. The most unlikely-seeming materials may help you create the most successful titles. For example, the interesting texture in "Flowers in Our Garden" comes from children's finger paints.

There's nothing more to this kind of title than a photographic color print of your favorite youngster and some wooden or plastic letters. For a way of animating the letters, see page 176.

The background was created with finger paints on waxed paper. It was placed on a concrete walk in bright sun and, as the camera ground away, someone dropped the blossoms, one at a time.

Trace your starting point and destination on a road map. Spell out the words you want with letters from a word game. You'll have a title that shows "who" and "where" at the same time.

This title consists of triangles of colored paper, wooden letters, and a couple of carnations. Such titles can be laid out on the floor and photographed with your light bar attached to the camera.

On a card of the size required by a movie titler, the text was "printed" in a typewriter. The artwork was then simply cut from sheets of colored paper and pasted down for filming in the titler.

With the camera shooting down at the floor, its light bar attached, various printed souvenirs of New York City were dropped, one at a time, to create a pleasantly informal pattern.

Many varied materials can be employed as backgrounds for wooden or plastic letters. Wood and wallpaper are two interesting possibilities. Here a portion of a matchstick bamboo drape was used.

139

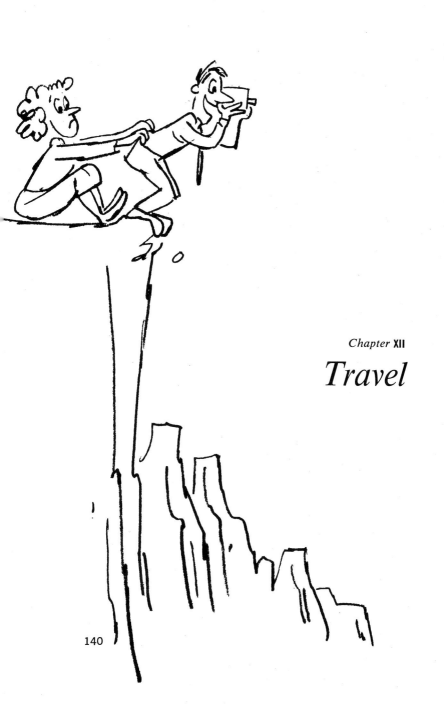

Chapter **XII**

Travel

For better travel movies, invent things for people to do, so they don't stand staring at the camera.

It's been known to rain on vacations. Our advice: Keep shooting anyway. You may never return to the spot you're visiting. You'll be surprised at how good your movies will be.

Filming Your Travels

Nothing recalls the color, fun, and excitement of your vacation trips like well-made movies. Golfers swing, kids dive into swimming pools, boats flash by, and things *happen* on the screen. Movies are the nearest thing to life itself.

It would be wrong to say that it's *easy* to get really good movie coverage of a trip. If you like moviemaking, the experience will be enjoyable. But it *does* take some time and thought to produce top-notch results. The things that make any movies fun to see also apply to your travel films. But there are a few differences.

Colorful subjects make colorful movies. Good photographers deliberately choose bright clothing and props for their movies.

Plan Ahead!

One important difference between backyard shooting and travel filming is pre-planning. You can shoot backyard footage pretty casually. You're on familiar ground. If the weather isn't just right, you can usually wait until another day. Not so with movies of your travels. On a trip, you're suddenly in a strange new place. The excellence of your results depends heavily on how well you've planned your shooting before ever leaving home. To help you plan intelligently, learn about the places you plan to visit. If you're headed for a national park, request a brochure describing its features from the park headquarters. Send for pamphlets from the local Chambers of Commerce of the places you plan to visit. Read about your vacation area in such magazines as *Holiday* and *National Geographic,* as well as in commercial travel guides available for most popular vacation spots.

The object of all this "homework" is to know what you want to shoot before you even get where you're going. *Even if you never expose a foot of film, this familiarity with your destination will help you enjoy your trip far, far more than if you arrive "cold."*

On the basis of the maps and facts you accumulate, plan a realistic schedule for the things you want to see—and photograph. Realistic is the key word. Don't try too much or you'll come back home exhausted. One European visitor to America, unaware of the vast distances involved, is said to have planned a shopping tour of Chicago one morning, followed by a picnic at the Grand Canyon in the afternoon, and a stop at Disneyland the same night!

All this scheduling may sound a little regimented, but you'll actually see more and get more pictures by sticking to some kind of schedule than by wandering aimlessly without a plan. If you have lots of time, that's a different story. But for most people, with only a few weeks of vacation to play with, planning ahead pays big dividends. Once you've made your plan, stick with it. Take pictures no matter what the weather's like. You'll be strongly tempted to say to yourself, "I'll come back tomorrow and shoot when it's sunny." Forget it. You won't be back— maybe ever again. Shoot while you're there. The author once filmed Alaska from Ketchikan to Point Barrow in three weeks. It rained every single day in every single spot. But the movies themselves are quite acceptable. And the rain itself became the film's "running gag."

What to Shoot

Some movie books tell you to capture the whole story of your trip by including close-ups of a hand locking the door of your house, people getting into the car, and so on. This is good but highly impractical advice. Anyone with a family knows the near-impossibility of being so organized at the moment of truth when a trip begins. If you simply get away without forgetting to turn the stove off, you're doing well.

What *should* you shoot, then? A few shots of how you traveled are appropriate—some pictures through the windshield of a moving car, or out the window of an airplane, for example. *Don't* shoot out the *side* window of a bus, car, or train. Scenery rushing by at high speed will be little more than an eye-tugging blur on the film. You can minimize the bumpiness of movies made from any moving vehicle by using a wide-angle lens (or the wide-angle position on your zoom lens).

You won't get much memorable footage from the window of a commercial airliner, except at low altitudes. Sit on the shady side of the plane. Don't let the camera touch any part of the plane; it will increase vibration in the camera if you brace your lens against the window, for example. Using an ultraviolet or skylight filter helps cut down the bluishness that's so apparent in color movies made from the air.

The real key to the success of your travel film will be what you shoot *after* you arrive. One "must," as we have already indicated in the section on titling, is signs. Shoot all kinds of signs and markers for colorful, ready-made movie titles.

Another must is lots of close-ups. Nothing will make your pictures more interesting than lots of close-ups. This is the voice of experience speaking. Most people concentrate on grand scenic views, distant buildings and monuments, snow-capped mountains, and other sweeping scenes. A little of this goes a long way. Instead, concentrate on close-ups of hands weaving rugs or making pottery or carving totem poles. Get

143

close-ups of faces and costumes and fishing tackle and outboard motors and anything else involved in your trip. Get in close more often than you're used to doing. Even a fixed-focus movie camera will let you get at least as close as three feet in bright sunlight. Take advantage of this fact. You'll be delighted at the results. (So will everyone else who sees your films.)

If you travel abroad, there are extra considerations of film availability, processing, and customs to think about. Tips on these matters, plus much more, appear in the KODAK Publication *Planning and Taking Your Travel Pictures,* sold where you bought this.

When You Travel Abroad

When you tread on foreign soil, many things change abruptly, but none of them alter the motions you go through to make a good movie.

The differences you'll encounter will be largely differences in supplying yourself with movie film and arranging to have that film processed. Customs regulations governing the amount of film you can carry duty-free from one country to another aren't entirely uniform, and individual customs officers often exercise considerable latitude in interpreting them. A friendly, co-operative attitude on your part in your relations with customs authorities can often move mountains.

If you're planning a junket on the continent, you'll find Kodak sales organizations ready to help you in almost every major country in the world.

Here are a few basic considerations which may influence the photographic logistics for any trip you plan:

• KODACHROME *II Movie Films sold abroad have the cost of processing included in the purchase price. Should you wish to have any of this film processed at a Kodak Laboratory in the United States, it will be done at no additional charge.*

• *Some countries have strict import regulations affecting color film and it is the customs officers of these nations who may object to your entry with large quantities of this film. It may be possible to overcome these objections by suggesting that*

144

the officer package and seal all of your film except the few rolls you plan to shoot in his country. You would then be unable to use any film from this package until you left.

- *Color film should not be kept for long periods between exposure and processing, especially under hot, humid conditions. If your stay abroad lasts about four weeks or less, there's relatively little risk in keeping your exposed film with you and sending it in for processing upon your return home. If you plan to be away longer, make some processing arrangements with your Kodak dealer before you leave so that you can either forward film to him from wherever you'll be or, with a KODAK Processing Mailing Label, send it to a Kodak Laboratory which, in turn, will send it to him. He can either hold the film for you, and perhaps send you a card every now and then to assure you that your camera is operating satisfactorily, or, if you have a fixed itinerary, return it to you abroad. If, however, you'll be moving around at a pretty rapid rate, it's inadvisable to plan on having your film returned to you en route unless you allow an extremely generous safety margin.*

- KODACHROME *II Movie Film is available nearly everywhere in the world. There are Kodak Processing Laboratories in many countries, but they cannot send your processed film to you at a United States address or at an address in any country but their own without some special arrangements being made.*

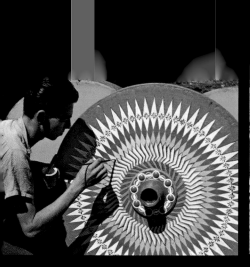
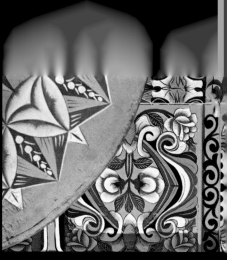

Wherever you travel, remember to photograph local sports, handicrafts, and ways of dressing, traveling, and living. And be sure to include lots of closeups.

MOVIES EN ROUTE

Once you actually reach wherever it is that you're going abroad, there's usually a seemingly endless supply of prospective subject matter for your movie camera. But the enjoyable business of getting there often presents some equally engaging movie material. Keeping your camera at hand may turn out to be very much worth while.

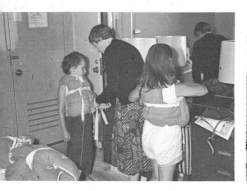

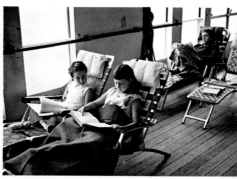

Chapter XIII

Special Techniques

Movie Tricks

A home-movie camera has more potential tricks in it than a magician's derby. An entire book might be written on this subject alone. In fact, several have. Generally, the more complex and versatile a camera is, the greater the range of legerdemain it is capable of producing, but even the simplest cameras, without single-framing provisions, slow-motion speeds, and built-in masking devices, can create remarkable effects.

One of the easiest stunts is to make people disappear. Starting with the camera on a firm support, photograph part of an activity and then, cautioning everyone in it to freeze, stop the camera. Hustle one of your subjects out of the picture, make no other changes, and begin shooting again. When you project the film, it will seem as if there's been a complete vanishing act.

A variation on this technique, one widely employed in silent movie comedies, is to have one person appear to transform himself into another. This is generally accomplished with the aid of a large tree. Someone walks right up to and behind the tree. You immediately cease shooting when most of his body becomes hidden by the tree. Then whisk him out of this location and stage someone else behind the tree. As you start shooting once more, this actor should stride out briskly, moving in the same direction as the previous participant. In your projected movie, the transformation will seem instantaneous.

Another application employs the services of the neighborhood small fry, the more of them the better. Place a large box or barrel in the middle of your scene and have one child climb out of it and walk away. Stop shooting and put another child into the box. Photograph the same action again. You can keep this up endlessly, and the box, in your film, will seem to yield an army of moppets. If you wish, you can work the trick in reverse by having the kids climb into the box. After about six or eight have done so, direct the next few to do a good deal of squirming around as they get inside, so that the box seems to be extremely crowded. When the final child walks up to the box, instead of having him get in, let him push it over, straining manfully, of course. Out might march a small dog or kitten.

Another wondrous trick is to have divers come zooming out of the water onto a diving board or boys appear to jump heights that are beyond the capabilities of Olympians. This can be managed by holding the camera upside down while you photograph a diver or a boy leaping *off* a fence. Then, after processing, the section of film should be cut out of the reel, turned top to bottom, and spliced back in. This reverses the action. With 8mm film, to keep the perforations on the correct side, it's necessary not only to turn the film top to bottom but flop it over as well. This, however, may make it necessary to refocus the projector slightly during this scene and will cause any lettering in the picture to appear backwards.

With any camera capable of single framing, you can easily create the illusion of a hopped-up world gone mad. Simply plant the camera on a tripod or KODAK FLEXICLAMP and shoot some activity as a string of single frames, one right after the other, just as quickly as you can make them. The result will be a pace wild enough to make even the Keystone Cops dizzy.

As a sure antidote to apathetic audiences, treat them to a scene in which someone washing a car turns around, notices the camera, picks up his bucket of water, and hurls its contents directly at the lens. The trick is to keep the camera behind a sheet of glass during the shooting.

With a little carpentry, you can also provide wings for your movie camera. First, cut a piece of scrap wood to about the same size as the bottom of your camera. Drill a hole in it large enough for the tripod screw and countersink an area on the bottom so that the tripod screw can get through to the camera to fasten it to the wood. Next, attach this piece of wood to a five-foot length of 2-by-4. For the actual shooting, start by

When a gray-coated boy runs behind a tree and turns into a red-coated girl, that's a good trick. It's also a rather easy one. With the camera on a tripod, stop shooting as soon as the boy is hidden. Replace him with the girl and begin filming again just as she starts to run out and be visible.

Obviously there's room in the barrel for only one child. To try convincing your audience this isn't so, mount your camera on a tripod and stop shooting after each child emerges. Then put another child in. For utmost realism, have the outside kids hold still whenever you stop the camera.

152

holding the entire apparatus steady and locking the camera button into the "on" position. Then, lift the 2-by-4 slowly and swing it in any direction you wish. The movies obtained will give the impression that gravity has lost all control of the camera. For best results, use a wide-angle lens or lens converter.

Fades

A fade-out at the end of a scene makes the picture become gradually dimmer until the screen is left entirely darkened. It's a neat way of indicating the close of a day in your movie story or the end of the film itself, or even of just a certain activity.

Really good outdoor fades can be produced only with cameras that employ an iris diaphragm to vary the size of the lens opening. The BROWNIE Movie Cameras and several other types use a rotating wheel with holes of various sizes in it that turns in front of the lens. Although these cameras cannot make a satisfactory fade outdoors, they can produce one indoors.

To fade-out an outdoor scene, while you are shooting, slowly

With a camera having an iris diaphragm, a fade-out such as this one can be performed by slowly turning the lens opening collar to the smallest opening while you continue to shoot. Once you've reached the smallest opening, place one hand over the lens and shoot for another second or two.

turn toward the smallest aperture the collar that sets the lens. This gradually reduces the amount of light reaching the film. After you reach the smallest opening, cover the lens with your hand and keep shooting for a second. It's easiest to accomplish this, of course, when your camera is sitting on a tripod, but with practice and a little dexterity the trick can be performed under hand-held operating conditions. With diaphragm-type lenses, this same system applies indoors.

There is another method, though, that can be used indoors with any kind of camera. Have someone take a pair of large cards, a foot square or bigger, and slowly move them in front of the photoflood lamps on your light bar while you keep operating the camera. This accomplishes the same purpose.

Fade-ins to begin a movie or some portion of a movie are achieved by reversing the fade-out technique.

Extreme Close-Ups

The shorter the distance from camera to subject, the larger the subject appears. Occasionally, being able to shoot at extremely close range is an invaluable asset, especially if your interests run to horticulture, scale-model railroads, or any other field in which tiny detail is of vast importance. Every camera, though, whether its lens be of the focusing or fixed-focus type, can approach only so near to a subject. Past this close-focusing limit —and it varies from one type of lens to another—the subject will photograph increasingly fuzzy and indistinct.

The close-focusing limit can be moved closer by the use of close-up lenses. These optical units, designed to be mounted like filters over the camera lens, are available in three powers: 1+, 2+, and 3+. The 3+ lens permits the shortest camera-to-subject distance—shorter than 8 inches on some cameras. Like filters, close-up lenses should be requested by series number and must be held with an adapter ring.

Focusing-type lenses on many 8mm and 16mm cameras can be adjusted to photograph subjects only 12 inches away. At this range, the lens "sees" an area only about 3 by 4 inches. With cameras capable of such extreme close-up shooting, the 1+ and 2+ lenses offer relatively slight advantage. The 3+ lens, however, allows camera-to-subject distances ranging from about 7½ inches to 13 inches, depending upon the focus setting of the camera lens.

But fixed-focus lenses on 8mm movie cameras permit you to shoot from no closer to a subject than about 3 feet at lens settings you normally use on a sunny day. At this distance, the lens "sees" an area about 12 by 15 inches. The table below shows how close you can get by using close-up lenses with a fixed-focus movie camera. Close-up lenses, however, must be removed from the camera when photographing more distant subjects.

When making movies with a close-up lens, the range of sharpness is extremely narrow and, when you have a 3+, it is virtually nonexistent. Actual distance measurements must be made. Estimates aren't accurate enough.

DATA ON CLOSE-UP LENSES WITH FIXED-FOCUS 8mm CAMERAS

Power of Close-up Lens	Range of Sharpness in Inches At Lens Setting of 8 (f8)		Area Covered by Lens in Inches At Lens Setting of 8 (f8)	
	From	To	Near	Far
1+	23	60	5½x7	15x20
2+	14	24½	3½x4¾	6⅛x8¼
3+	10¼	15¼	2¾x3⅝	3⅞x5⅛

But there's an even greater complication to extreme close-up shooting. On most movie cameras, the viewfinder is a couple of inches above the camera lens and therefore doesn't see exactly the same area as the film sees. At normal shooting distances, this variance is so inconsequential that it can be entirely ignored. Only at about 3 feet and less does it become necessary to compensate for this parallax effect. Extremely short ranges, though, create a severe parallax problem. At 12 inches, only about the bottom half of the area visible through the finder appears in the movie frame. The remainder of the picture is below the area seen through the finder.

This makes it quite desirable to have a device that not only shows the correct camera-to-subject distance for a close-up lens

COLLECTORS' ITEMS

When small, colorful flowers fill large movie screens, something special usually happens. Audiences gasp. The gardener is filled with a new pride in his and nature's accomplishment. A great deal of footage of a garden as a whole is bland movie fare, but when you get in close, really close, the bright cameos you capture on film will be an ample reward for the effort.

157

but one that marks off the exact area the camera lens sees, so that viewfinding becomes unnecessary.

One of the simplest devices for accomplishing this end works beautifully and costs nothing. We call it a "focal board." It's simply a rectangle of cardboard—the kind the laundry puts in men's shirts works fine—with notches cut in one end. The distance from one end of the board to the notch at the other end shows how far the camera should be from the subject. The width of the notch shows how much of your subject will appear in the movie. A diagram for making such a focal board for both regular 8 and super 8 cameras appears on the next page. The figures shown are for a fixed-focus camera, or a focusing camera set at 15 feet. For other distances, use the figures in the tables below.

DATA ON CLOSE-UP LENSES FOR REGULAR 8mm CAMERAS
with focusing 13mm lenses

Camera Focus Scale Setting in Feet	Lens 2+		Lens 3+	
	Lens-to-Subject Distance in Inches	Area Covered By Lens in Inches	Lens-to-Subject Distance in Inches	Area Covered By Lens in Inches
INF.	$19\frac{1}{2}$	5x6$\frac{3}{4}$	13	3$\frac{3}{8}$x4$\frac{1}{2}$
50	$19\frac{1}{8}$	4$\frac{7}{8}$x6$\frac{1}{2}$	12$\frac{7}{8}$	3$\frac{3}{8}$x4$\frac{3}{8}$
25	$18\frac{1}{2}$	4$\frac{3}{4}$x6$\frac{3}{8}$	12$\frac{1}{2}$	3$\frac{1}{4}$x4$\frac{3}{8}$
15*	$17\frac{3}{4}$	4$\frac{5}{8}$x6$\frac{1}{8}$	12$\frac{1}{4}$	3$\frac{1}{4}$x4$\frac{1}{4}$
10	$16\frac{7}{8}$	4$\frac{3}{8}$x5$\frac{7}{8}$	11$\frac{7}{8}$	3$\frac{1}{8}$x4$\frac{1}{8}$
8	$16\frac{3}{8}$	4$\frac{1}{4}$x5$\frac{5}{8}$	11$\frac{1}{2}$	3x4
6	$15\frac{1}{2}$	4x5$\frac{3}{8}$	11$\frac{1}{8}$	2$\frac{7}{8}$x3$\frac{7}{8}$
4	14	3$\frac{5}{8}$x4$\frac{7}{8}$	10$\frac{3}{8}$	2$\frac{5}{8}$x3$\frac{1}{2}$
3	$12\frac{5}{8}$	3$\frac{1}{4}$x4$\frac{3}{8}$	9$\frac{1}{2}$	2$\frac{1}{2}$x3$\frac{3}{8}$
2	$10\frac{1}{2}$	2$\frac{3}{4}$x3$\frac{5}{8}$	8$\frac{1}{4}$	2$\frac{1}{4}$x3

*The data for 15 feet apply to fixed-focus 8mm movie cameras.

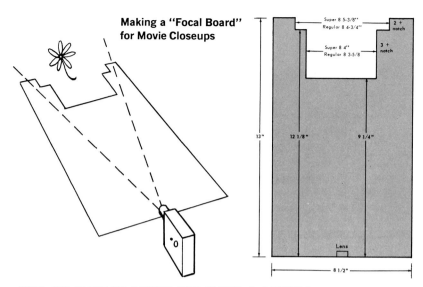

Making a "Focal Board" for Movie Closeups

Super 8 5-3/8"
Regular 8 4-3/4"

2 + notch

Super 8 4"
Regular 8 3-5/8

3 + notch

13" 12 1/8" 9 1/4"

Lens

8 1/2"

DATA ON CLOSE-UP LENSES FOR SUPER 8 CAMERAS

with focusing 13mm lenses

Camera Focus Scale Setting in Feet	Lens 2+		Lens 3+	
	Lens-to-Subject Distance in Inches	Area Covered By Lens in Inches	Lens-to-Subject Distance in Inches	Area Covered By Lens in Inches
INF.	$19\frac{1}{2}$	$6\frac{1}{8}$x$8\frac{1}{4}$	13	$4\frac{1}{8}$x$5\frac{1}{2}$
50	$19\frac{1}{8}$	6x$7\frac{7}{8}$	$12\frac{7}{8}$	$4\frac{1}{8}$x$5\frac{3}{8}$
25	$18\frac{1}{2}$	$5\frac{3}{4}$x$7\frac{3}{4}$	$12\frac{1}{2}$	4x$5\frac{3}{8}$
15	$17\frac{3}{4}$	$5\frac{5}{8}$x$7\frac{1}{2}$	$12\frac{1}{4}$	4x$5\frac{1}{4}$
10	$16\frac{7}{8}$	$5\frac{3}{8}$x$7\frac{1}{4}$	$11\frac{7}{8}$	$3\frac{7}{8}$x5
8	$16\frac{3}{8}$	5x$6\frac{7}{8}$	$11\frac{1}{2}$	$3\frac{5}{8}$x$4\frac{7}{8}$
6	$15\frac{1}{2}$	$4\frac{7}{8}$x$6\frac{1}{2}$	$11\frac{1}{8}$	$3\frac{1}{2}$x$4\frac{3}{4}$
4	14	$4\frac{3}{8}$x6	$10\frac{3}{8}$	$3\frac{1}{4}$x$4\frac{1}{4}$
3	$12\frac{5}{8}$	4x$5\frac{3}{8}$	$9\frac{1}{2}$	3x4
2	$10\frac{1}{2}$	$3\frac{3}{8}$x$4\frac{5}{8}$	$8\frac{1}{4}$	$2\frac{3}{4}$x$3\frac{5}{8}$

159

Animation

A girl in a movie jumps rope, and her action seems smooth and continuous. Examine the reel of film, though, and you see a long string of individual pictures like tiny color snapshots. In each of them, the girl's position is slightly different because she's moved somewhat in the intervals between the pictures.

The only major difference between this sort of ordinary movie action and animated movies is that the subject matter in animation isn't inherently capable of motion. It's necessary for you, then, to shoot a single frame of the subject; change its position very slightly and shoot another single frame.

As far as making single-frame exposures is concerned, nearly all 16mm cameras and many 8mm cameras have provisions for

The letters are added to the background picture one at a time and, with the camera fixed in position, two or three frames are exposed at each addition. When projected, the title seems to write itself.

Place a toy car on a map at the same place where you started a trip. Shoot one frame. Move the car slightly along your route and shoot another. Draw a red line behind the car to show the route. When the film is projected, the car seems to move by its own power.

160

doing this. On most of them, exposing a frame at a time is achieved by pressing the camera button in the direction opposite to the one in which you press it for ordinary movies. Single framing can be performed, though, even with cameras like those in the BROWNIE Movie series, which aren't specifically designed to do it. By merely flicking the button lightly with the tip of your finger, you'll generally be able to expose only one or two frames at a time.

By animation, you can produce a title that seems to write itself. Start with a sheet of solid-color poster paper spread on the floor and a set of wooden letters. Mount your camera on a tripod, a requirement for all animation work, and point it down at the paper. For illumination, use your light bar. The title might be "Gerry's Baby Days." First, shoot one or two seconds' worth of the plain sheet of colored paper, as you would an ordinary movie. Then, lay the "G" on it and expose two frames. Add the second letter and shoot two more frames. Just continue this until the entire title is down. Then make about three seconds of ordinary movies of the complete title and, when projected, the words will spell out quite magically.

To title a movie of a motor trip, you could show a toy car covering the route on a road map. Again, begin by placing the map on the floor and setting up your camera and lights. Shoot about two seconds of regular movies of the map alone, preferably with your starting point at the very edge of the picture. Then put the car at the starting point and shoot one frame. Advance it slightly along your route and shoot another. In the projected scene, the car will appear to travel along under its own power. You can add a little extra fun by having it seem to bump along. For one frame, tip the front of the car up slightly by placing something under it. For the next, move it forward a little and this time prop up its back end.

For singleframing, be sure that the camera is set at 16 frames per second and that you use a lens opening one full setting *smaller* than you normally would for the distance from lights to subject. For example, if the exposure table in the film instructions recommended a setting of 8, you would use a setting of 11 for all single-frame animation shots you choose to make.

Chapter XIV

Care of Your Camera and Film

Camera Maintenance

A movie camera, like a camel, will go a long way with very little attention. The few spots that should be checked from time to time are:

THE LENS: If there are any dirt or fingerprints on the lens, wipe the surface gently with either a lens tissue or a clean, soft, lintless cloth. By wrapping your cleaning material around a wooden matchstick, you will be able to get at the edges. Removable lenses should be unscrewed to allow occasional cleaning of the rear face.

THE GATE: Any dirt, hair, or scraps of film that adhere to the gate can create dark marks around the edges of your movies and, perhaps, scratch them. Consult your camera instruction booklet for the correct method of removing the pressure plate. When you have it out of the camera, wipe both it and the aperture plate with a slightly moist cloth and polish them dry with a soft, lintless cloth. Do not scrape either surface with any metallic object.

THE ELECTRIC MOTOR: If your camera has a built-in tester for the batteries that power its electric motor, be sure to check the batteries periodically, especially before a trip or other pro-

Use alkaline batteries in your movie camera, and replace them once a year. Keep the contacts bright and clean by rubbing them with a pencil eraser or a piece of rough cloth.

longed shooting session. If you don't have a built-in battery tester, it's a safe rule of thumb to replace your batteries once a year or after exposing 25 rolls of film, whichever comes first. (Tip: Put a small piece of tape on the camera or its case. Jot down on it the date you replace the batteries. Then you'll know when you're ready for new ones.)

Use the right *type* of batteries. Alkaline batteries are recommended for all KODAK electric-drive movie cameras. They have better shelf life and will run many more rolls of film through your camera than conventional zinc-carbon batteries. The only time you should *not* use alkaline batteries is when your equipment has unplated brass or copper battery contacts. Such contacts will corrode when used with alkaline cells. If your equipment has contacts of stainless steel or nickel plating (which will be silver in color), use alkaline cells for longer service.

If your camera will be idle for some time, remove the batteries to prevent corrosion damage. Keep both battery and camera contacts clean with a pencil eraser. Storing batteries in a freezer will extend their life. Wrap them in plastic for moisture protection.

Don't oil any part of your camera without first checking your instruction booklet. Many movie cameras are entirely prelubricated and never need oiling. Incorrect or unnecessary oiling can spoil your movies.

Consult your camera dealer about any repairs that you think may be required. Take a recent roll of your movies along if they seem adversely affected by improper functioning.

Caring for Your Film

The arch-foes of unprocessed movie film are high temperature and high humidity. An excess of either can garble the colors produced by color film and alter the exposure requirements of any film, black-and-white or color.

The humidity menace is almost entirely hobbled by the type of packaging in which Kodak supplies its movie films. All magazine loads, both 8mm and 16mm, are sealed in *water-vapor-tight* envelopes of foil and plastic; rolls come in cans sealed with *water-vapor-resistant* tape. In most areas of North America, both forms of packing are proof against humidity, but, if any film in vapor-resistant containers must be stored for a week or longer in some locality commonly having relative humidities of 70 percent or greater, the factory-applied tape should be reinforced with an additional layer of ordinary adhesive tape.

Under any circumstances, the original package shouldn't be broken until you are ready to load the film into your camera.

Temperature troubles can be avoided by storing film in some part of your home not likely to become much warmer than 70 degrees. If you plan to keep any film for longer than four weeks, especially in hot summer months, place the unopened package on the bottom shelf of your refrigerator. Rolls of movie film should be sealed in a dry, rubber-sealed jar to protect them from the high humidity level. Remove the film from the refrigerator an hour or two in advance of use so that it may reach outside temperature.

Once you have loaded a roll or magazine of film into your camera, make sure, then, that the camera isn't subjected to extremes of either heat or humidity or both. Never leave it on the rear deck, in the glove compartment, or in the trunk of an automobile.

The briefer the length of time a roll of film remains in your camera, the better. If you expose a dozen feet of film at one time and then finish the roll several months later, chances are that there will be a noticeable difference in color quality between the two sections. Not only should a roll or magazine of film be exposed over a fairly brief period of time, but the film should be processed as soon as possible after being taken from the camera.

Processed film is vulnerable to not only heat and humidity but to strong light as well. Light can affect the dyes which form the color in color movies. Keep your films out of attics and basements and away from heating pipes. Moisture is an especial hazard since it may cause fungus growths on the film. A 200-foot reel and reel can for 8mm movies cost less than two dollars and offer an inexpensive way of protecting irreplaceable films from light.

Should any finger marks or dirt become attached to your movies, the most effective means of cleaning them is by passing the film lightly through a pad of cotton nearly saturated with KODAK Movie Film Cleaner (with Lubricant).

Chapter XV

Projection

Screens

A matte projection screen does not provide as brilliant a picture as a beaded screen, but the picture on it can be viewed from farther to the side. With a beaded screen, all of your audience should be seated inside an arc of forty degrees, measured from the center of the screen; with a matte surface, the angle can be sixty degrees. Another type of screen surface, called lenticular, combines brightness with a wide viewing angle.

Any screen should be erected in the darkest possible location and be high enough so that it is visible to the viewers in the rear row. It is especially important that no stray light strike a beaded screen from behind the audience. If you have a matte screen, make certain that there's no light near it during a showing.

The screen must be perpendicular to the projector. If it isn't, the picture image will stretch into a distorted form. This should be checked when you set up the screen and projector rather than after your audience is at hand.

Screens generally demand very little special maintenance. The beaded type may tend to become dusty after a while, due to the coarseness of its surface. In general, dusting should be performed with an extremely soft brush of the kind used on babies' hair. Stiff bristles may remove the beaded finish. If a beaded screen becomes spotted, consult either the screen instructions or the screen manufacturer.

Dust can be removed from a matte surface also with a soft brush. Most matte screens may be cleaned with a damp cloth.

Silent Projectors

A movie projector should be situated far enough away from the screen so that, if at all possible, its picture fills the entire screen area. It should also be high enough for its beam to clear the heads of the audience. If a projector is considerably beneath screen level, distortion will probably occur.

Always have your projector ready to go before your audience files in. Start by cleaning its lens gently with a lens tissue or a soft, relatively lint-free cloth. Every once in a while, the projector's film gate — the place at which each frame is actually projected — needs to be wiped, too. Your instruction booklet will show how.

When you connect your projector to an electrical outlet, wind its cord several turns around the leg of the table on which it is sitting. If anyone should then accidentally trip over the cord in the darkness, the projector won't be seriously damaged. Thread the projector and run some film through. This gives you an opportunity to focus and to level. Once you've done both, stop the projector and reverse the film until you reach the very beginning of the reel. Stop it again, and you're all prepared to launch a showing without any pause or irritating delay.

When you project more than one reel, don't do any rewinding until all have been projected. With rented films, the company from which you rent may prefer that you not rewind at all. At the end of a showing, turn the projection lamp off, but let the motor continue running for a few minutes to cool the projector.

On the new prelubricated projectors, maintenance may amount to no more than keeping the lens and film gate clean. Certainly, before applying oil to any part of a projector, consult the instruction booklet. To a prelubricated machine, oiling can be quite harmful, and to one that isn't prelubricated, incorrect application can be equally damaging.

Once your projection lamp begins to blacken, it should be replaced even though it may still seem to provide a fairly considerable amount of illumination.

Should your projector not operate correctly and you cannot, yourself, diagnose the difficulty, return it to your dealer. He may be able to correct the problem or will send it to either the manufacturer's service department or some reliable independent organization.

Sound Projection

Sound projection has some unique wrinkles. One of the most important is that you should warm up the amplifier before you start running a film. If you commence with a cold amplifier and adjust the volume to suit it, when the system does warm up it will bang out a thunderous "Anvil Chorus" on your eardrums. Modern sound projectors may have transistorized amplifiers that require no warm-up.

When setting up screen and projector, the speaker should be located fairly near the screen and at screen level. Either keep it entirely away from any walls or place it in a corner. Test the sound system and adjust the volume at the same time as you attend to the focus and leveling. When your audience enters, then, you can immediately show movies without any tedious dial twiddling.

Amplifier tubes ought to be tested twice a year and defective ones replaced. If both your projection lamp and amplifier ever cut out, check the power supply. If only the sound fails, investigate the speaker cord at the jack that connects it to the amplifier. Trace any amplifier difficulties as directed in your projector instruction booklet.

Sound films are usually made at 24 frames per second rather than 16, and the projector must be operated at higher speed.

Adding Sound to Your Movies

Only the most taciturn individual ever has a truly silent movie. Nearly every showing of every film is accompanied by some sort of oral commentary, usually supplied by its creator. Orally,

168

of course, is the very easiest way of adding sound.

Background music via phonograph or tape recordings is an added refinement. Although it's quite desirable to have the music originate from alongside the screen, this usually turns out to be a rather inconvenient location, at least to whomever is operating the projector. If, in your arsenal of audio equipment, you have an extension speaker, you might locate this up front, but keep the remainder of the paraphernalia alongside the projector. For an added touch, especially if you're an electrical gadgeteer, a microphone could be wired into the circuit so that your comments will also emanate from the speaker.

One of the great obstacles in this sort of hookup is the length of the recordings. While a certain piece of music may be entirely appropriate to scenes of skiers whipping over a slope, it's probably out of character for, say, a late-evening party at the ski lodge. If you have the luxury of two turntables, you can overcome a good bit of this problem by switching from one to another, but a tape recorder will solve it a great deal more conveniently.

With a recorder and a phonograph, you can prepare a special tape to accompany the showing of any of your films. A certain musical selection may be made to last only as long as the scenes it fits. You can even add sound effects. Exact synchronization isn't at all essential. Your camera dealer can probably advise you of some sources of sound effects recordings.

For a zany touch, a movie-plus-taped-sound can be assembled so that all of the noises are intentionally ridiculous. A scene showing a steamship's great whistle might be accompanied by a fifelike trill; a view of a great waterfall, by a drip-drip-drip from the kitchen faucet.

The ultimate achievement is the addition of a complete sound track directly on an 8mm, super 8, or 16mm film. Present 8mm and 16mm magnetic sound projectors make it easy and economical to make sound movies from any of your existing footage. In this system, the film is striped along one edge with a material similar to that used on magnetic tape. Kodak's coating of this kind is called "SONOTRACK" and is available through your usual sources of Kodak processing. It can even be applied to 16mm films which already have a conventional optical sound track, so that either the magnetic or optical track can be played for a given performance. Your Kodak dealer will be happy to demonstrate sound projectors for you.

Once the magnetic coating has been applied, the film can be run through a magnetic-type sound projector. While it is being projected, a very simple or a fairly complex sound track can be applied. It's possible to feed background music onto the stripe. You can add sound effects, either from a recording or through the microphone. On top of this, a vocal commentary can be transcribed. Just as with ordinary tape recording, any errors can be wiped out and corrected. You can re-record on the same film as often as you wish.

Movies that are going to have magnetic sound tracks should, preferably, be exposed at 24 frames per second since the sound, then, will have better fidelity. Sound, however, can be recorded at 16 frames per second for films shot at that camera speed.

Magnetic sound films should be edited before the addition of the striping, not only because this will turn out to be more economical but also because there is a possibility that, when a splicer is used on striped film, its steel scraper and cutter may become magnetized. Should this occur, a noticeable click will be heard through the speaker during projection every time a splice travels through the sound head.

Some film cleaners have a tendency to soften magnetic sound stripings. As a precaution, test any you are planning to use on the end of the film before applying it generally.

Index